VICKERS BARROW BUILT WARSHIPS
by Jon Wise

HMS Andrew on a sunny April day in 1946 having just been launched into the Walney Channel. The boat was the last of the Barrow built A Class to reach this stage. No fewer than 46 of these submarines were originally projected, of which Barrow was to receive contracts for 21, but priorities changed and in the end only sixteen were built. Vickers, with a final order for ten, received the lion's share. In order to demonstrate the effectiveness of the schnorkel system, **HMS Andrew** was selected to undertake what became a record fifteen day, submerged, trans-Atlantic crossing from Bermuda to England in 1953. As well as providing excellent PR for the Royal Navy the event was timed to coincide with the Coronation of Queen Elizabeth II. *(The Dock Museum Cat. No. 2365)*

Foreword

As I write, another significant chapter has just been added to the proud history of Barrow shipbuilding, with the naming and roll-out of the first Astute class submarine on 8 June, 2007, by Her Royal Highness The Duchess of Cornwall. This was a magnificent occasion that began a weekend of celebration, not only for the workforce, but also for our partners in the Royal Navy and Ministry of Defence, our sub contractors and the families and community whose support is such a vital part of the shipyard's successes. The design and construction of this nuclear-powered submarine represents the most complex undertaking in the UK today and without the overwhelming support, commitment and in many cases, personal sacrifice of the workforce and their families we could not have achieved this splendid occasion.

It is this dedication and community support, in addition to the skills, expertise and craftsmanship, that are behind the Barrow shipyard's worldwide reputation for building the finest ships and submarines, many of which you will see on the following pages. Jon is absolutely right to highlight the importance to the nation of retaining the engineering expertise behind these magnificent vessels. Just as important is the unique relationship between the shipyard and the community, without which many of the achievements celebrated on these pages would not have been possible.

I am proud to have led such a dedicated workforce and been part of such a supporting community. As long as the nation recognises the importance of the skills and expertise built up here over the last century and more, and as long as that dedication of the workforce and support of the community provides such a potent force for achievement, Barrow will continue to produce submarines and ships of which the Royal Navy and the nation can be proud.

Murray Easton
Managing Director
BAE Systems Submarine Solutions

Acknowledgements

I am grateful for the help of Sabine Skae, Collections and Exhibitions Officer at the Dock Museum, Barrow-in-Furness for arranging access to the superb Vickers Archive and also Graham Cubbin who helped me to identify some key features in the selected photographs. I would like to thank Mike Vallance for his time and patience, not only providing me with images for the book from the official BAE Systems photographic archive but also for answering many of my questions. I would also like to thank Tony Salter-Ellis, BAE Systems Shipyards History and Heritage Representative for his invaluable input and advise. My thanks are also due to Murray Easton, Managing Director of BAE Systems Submarine Solutions, for providing the Foreword.

Finally, I am most indebted to Ken Royall, a long-time Barrow resident, who has smoothed several paths for me, been the source of many of the photographs and has furnished me with a good deal of background information about Barrow and its shipbuilding past. Ken has risked life and limb, not to mention the arm of the law, to photograph every vessel built by this firm since the 1950s and I am delighted that a selection of his fine work is reaching a wider audience here for the first time.

Jon Wise
November, 2008

Select Bibliography

T. Clark, *A Century of Shipbuilding: Products of Barrow-in-Furness* (Dalesman Books, 1971)

Alec Dancer, *The Dons Delivered* (Alec Dancer, 2002)

Norman Friedman, *British Destroyers & Frigates: The Second World War and After* (Chatham Publishing, 2006)

Nigel Harris editor, *Portrait of a Shipbuilder: Barrow-Built Vessels from 1873* (Silver Link Publishing Ltd., 1989)

Jack Hool & Keith Nutter, *Damned Un-English Machines: A History of Barrow-Built Submarines* (Tempus Publishing, 2003)

Andrew Gordon, '*Naval Procurement and Shipbuilding Capacity, 1918-1939*' in D.J. Starkey and Alan Jamieson, editors, *Exploiting the Sea: Aspects of British Maritime Economy since 1870* (Exeter University Press, 1998)

Lewis Johnman and Hugh Murphy, '*The Rationalisation of Warship Building in the United Kingdom, 1945-2000*' in *The Journal of Strategic Studies, Vol. 24, No. 3* (September 2001)

Alan Lockett, *The Man wants his Boat: Stories of Barrow Shipyard* (Trinity Press, 1995)

Captain J. E. Moore, RN, editor, *The Impact of Polaris: The Origins of Britain's Nuclear Deterrent* (Richard Netherwood Ltd., 1999)

J.S.Redshaw, *Ships: A Study in Modern Shipbuilding* (Frederick Muller, 1947)

J..D.Scott, *Vickers: A History* (Weidenfeld & Nicholson, 1962)

Fred M. Walker, *Steel Ship Building* (Shire Publications, 1981)

Vickers Barrow Built Warships

Barrow-in-Furness is sometimes described as being "at the end of the longest cul-de-sac in England". Its geographical isolation makes it unique in one respect: all other major British naval shipbuilders have been located within cities or conurbations whereas Barrow is essentially a medium-sized town surrounded by countryside.

Vickers, to apply a single title to a company which has evolved and changed its name a number of times since becoming Vickers, Sons and Maxim Limited in 1897, still dominates a significant part of the Barrow skyline today, particularly the large swathe of land between the docks and Walney Channel. Here, the strikingly broad streets, widened to facilitate the movement of very large items of equipment and prefabricated hull units, together with the imposing red sandstone industrial buildings, are as much a feature of the area as the housing estates of Vickerstown on nearby Walney Island which were specially built by the company for its workers at the dawn of the 20th Century.

Today, however, it would be harder for a casual visitor to detect that Barrow still has a key role to play in shipbuilding. The area fronting Walney Channel once occupied by the slipways, in constant use for over a century and formerly a very visual hub of activity, now bears few traces of its former usage. This is because the vast majority of the work is carried out literally behind closed doors within the immense Devonshire Dock Hall, a 25,000 square metre building which towers above the surrounding landscape. One of the outcomes of the switch from the traditional dynamic launch of a ship from a slipway to "dunking" by means of a synchronised shiplift, is that the vessel is visible to the general public and exposed to the vagaries of the weather for far less time. In the case of the latest submarine **HMS Astute**, for example, only about 15% of her total time under construction at Barrow will have taken place outside the build hall.

Vickers' pre-eminence in submarine building is the constant that links the beginning of both the 20th and 21st Centuries. One measure of the high regard with which it has been held for so long in that capacity is the fact that 28 "first of class" submarines have been built at Barrow out of a total of 38, excluding prototypes and "one-off" experimental boats.

The Swedish inventor Thorsten Nordenfelt ordered two submarines from the shipyard in 1885 when trading as the Barrow Shipbuilding Company and the first boat was launched the next year. The British Government's initial resistance to these submersibles, which it considered only to be useful to weaker nations for defensive purposes, lasted until 1900. This consensus view arose from the Admiralty's deliberate ploy to play down the potential of submersibles. To have given them more credence publicly would have prompted more navies to acquire them. At the time, Britain had a most powerful and dominant surface fleet and appreciated only too well what havoc unseen underwater weapons could wreak. Behind the scenes, the Government avidly followed the progress of every foreign experimental submersible; even helping to fund one that showed promise! But as soon as the Hollands being built in America were deemed a sufficiently credible weapon, the Government acted decisively by selecting JP Holland's latest as yet unbuilt design and ordering five from Vickers, Sons & Maxim. After that, Vickers was granted a total monopoly in Royal Navy submarine building. The agreement secured was for 25 years and related to design rights and licences. However, by 1910, concerns felt by the Government at having just one source of supply for submarines led to other yards becoming involved, principally Scotts of Greenock, Cammell Laird at Birkenhead and H.M. Dockyard, Chatham.

Sixty four submarines were launched at Barrow during World War I (1914-19). It is a measure of the increasing importance of undersea warfare that 39 of these entered the water in the period 1917-1919. The immediate post-war years proved to be a difficult time for British naval shipbuilding in general. The cancellation of the capital-ship programme in the aftermath of the 1923 Washington Treaty impacted on the naval heavy armaments industry in which Vickers-Armstrongs was deeply involved. When representatives, seeking investment for the town, lobbied the Government they pleaded that 'Barrow has been killed by the Washington Treaty'. However, in 1929, Vickers-Armstrongs' Board was reassured that the Admiralty had recognised the need to maintain the firm's unique industrial capacity as a builder of submarines by tacitly granting Vickers, Barrow and Chatham Dockyard what amounted to a monopoly in this sector.

Subsequent events prevented the creation of such an oligarchy but the firm did bear the brunt of the submarine construction programmes immediately before and during World War II. Over ninety Royal Navy submarines were launched at Barrow in the period 1937-45; amongst many famous names that have since passed into legend, **HMS Upholder** was sent down the ways in July 1940. The eight year building boom abruptly terminated in the summer of 1945; the end of the war brought the cancellation of over half Barrow's allocation of 'A' Class submarine orders.

In total, only 21 warships were completed in British yards in the period 1945-50; nine of these were Barrow-built submarines. The necessary expertise was maintained during the 1950s with orders for three of a new generation of quiet, diesel-electric boats of the Porpoise Class. Less well remembered nowadays is the company's involvement with the Admiralty Development Establishment, also located at Barrow, which resulted in the construction of two experimental Explorer Class submarines, *Explorer* and *Excalibur*, fitted with high-test peroxide (HTP) driven steam turbines. In the late 1940s, with nuclear propulsion still a fairly distant prospect, HTP had seemed to offer at least a mid-term solution to the requirement for a fast and, possibly, a true submarine.

Towards the end of the decade, Vickers was handed responsibility for building the first nuclear-powered submarine which was to incorporate the US-designed Westinghouse S5W nuclear reactor. This was probably a foregone conclusion as the company had been involved in the development of Britain's prototype nuclear propulsion plant since 1955. An effective monopoly in submarine construction was eventually resumed in the middle of the following decade and, by 1971, Vickers had been designated the sole supplier of nuclear-powered submarines for the Royal Navy. Subsequently, all the Royal Navy's nuclear boats have been built by Vickers at Barrow.

Although the nuclear submarine represented an opportunity for the country to produce its first 'capital ships' to be designed since the war, there was a significant down side to this achievement. They were expensive – **HMS Dreadnought** cost £18.5 million, **HMS Warspite** of the follow-on Valiant Class, £21.5 million and the first Fleet Ballistic Submarine, **HMS Resolution,** £40.2 million. These huge amounts necessarily impacted on the rest of the Naval budget at a time when Britain was suffering from its worst peacetime balance of payments deficit. Amongst the casualties, as the new Labour Government's attempted to address the problem, was the CVA-01 carrier project.

The country's international market share in shipbuilding was in sharp decline at this time; between 1963-71 the number of ship launches in British yards fell from 12% to just 5% of the world's total. In the mean time, the Admiralty had abandoned its long-term policy of maintaining construction capacity within the naval yards and of contra-cyclical building (automatically ordering warships when there was a slump in merchant shipping demand) in favour of competitive tendering and the pursuit of value for money. Shipbuilders with composite mercantile/naval portfolios suffered the most while a still latent over-capacity in the naval sector required the Government to step in to save Cammell Laird, Harland and Wolff and Govan from closure in the early 1970s.

Vickers' secure position as a specialist submarine builder stood the company in good stead at this juncture. When the decision was taken to construct the Resolution Class SSBNs at Barrow and at Birkenhead, serious concerns were expressed about the problems of moving such large, deep vessels through the shallow waters of the Walney Channel and the busy River Mersey. Devonport Dockyard became a contender as an alternative building facility. Significantly, Vickers won the day because it was concluded that work had to be placed where the specialised submarine skills already existed and this key consideration was still pertinent a quarter of a century later when the decision was taken to build the entire Vanguard Class at Barrow.

The 2006 White Paper on the future of the UK's Independent Strategic Nuclear Deterrent, which confirmed the Government's intention that the Trident successor would be again be borne by a submarine and that it would be built in Britain, appears to have ensured the long-term future of this highly specialist workforce. However, two salutory lessons were demonstrated by the near collapse in 2002 of the follow-on to the Vanguard programme, the Astute Class SSN build. Firstly, there was the absolute necessity to retain a core of design and engineering expertise. This expertise included designers experienced at submarine work, specialised teams for loading the reactor into the hull, nuclear design staff for the reactor itself and the skills necessary to retain the nuclear site licence.

The second lesson reflected the sheer pace of technological change and the readiness to abandon existing working practices. *Astute* was the first submarine to be built at Barrow employing computer-aided design (CAD) using a three-dimensional model. This new system of working had not been properly developed when it was first used on this project. Moreover, the contract had been negotiated on a fixed-price basis, with all responsibility for the design and build resting with the owners, at that time GEC. Such was the sheer complexity of this engineering task, comprising, as it did, over one million individual component parts, that wholesale changes had to be adopted when BAE Systems acquired GEC in 1999. Murray Easton, the current Manager Director of BAE Submarine Solutions, holds the view that, 'if things hadn't changed, the MoD would have cancelled the Astute programme and there would be no submarines in the navy'.

Of course, Vickers has also constructed a large number of surface ships for the Royal Navy although it has not dominated this sector of the "market" to nearly the same extent as it has with submarines. It has only built six battleships and battle-cruisers, for example, the last being **HMS Revenge** which was launched in 1915. Apart from the two War Programme orders for **HMS Jamaica**, launched 1940, and *Spartan* (1942), it won contracts for just two other cruisers in the entire inter-war period.

On the other hand, only Harland & Wolff in Belfast has built more fleet carriers; both Vickers at Barrow and Swan Hunter have been responsible for five each. Vickers became the lead yard for the Illustrious Class, the nameship being laid down at Barrow in 1937, the same year as **HMS Indomitable** which was intended to be the fourth ship, but whose specification altered sufficiently during construction for her to be designated a separate class. Significantly, when a shortage of planning staff at the Royal Corps of Naval Constructors (RCNC) forced the Admiralty to hand over the basic requirements for the 1942 carrier project to Vickers, the result was the highly successful Colossus Class light fleet carrier design.

Lead yard responsibilities were again granted in the 1970s when the firm received the contract to build the carrier **HMS Invincible**. In this case it was recognised that Vickers was the only company with the resources to develop the RCNC Ship Department's design for the "first of class". By the same token, the company also built the first Type 42 destroyer, **HMS Sheffield**, which was launched in 1971 and the first of the "stretched" version, **Manchester**, which went down the ways nine years later. Finally, in July 1996, it was announced that both the Albion Class assault ships were to be constructed at Barrow and these two, plus **RFA Wave Knight**, were the first naval vessels to be launched into the Walney Channel from the so-called "super-berth".

The fact that Vickers has always been primarily a private, commercial concern (apart from a short period under state-ownership), operating in a highly competitive international market, is illustrated by the large number of naval vessels of all types it has built for other nations, an export record that spans most of the period covered by this book. Its naval customer list includes no fewer than seventeen different countries from Eastern Europe, the Near and Far East, South America and the Commonwealth.

The company's ability to design, launch and outfit large, sophisticated warships enabled countries which lacked the necessary indigenous skills to benefit both in the short and sometimes the long term. For example, Argentina was able to construct her second Type 42 destroyer, **ARA Santisima Trindad**, at AFNE, Rio de Santiago in the 1970s because they had not only witnessed the building of the first ship at Barrow but had also benefited from a sales package which included the provision of technical aid from Vickers back home in Argentina. Much earlier in the century, Japan's links with the company, which resulted in the construction of three major warships and two submarines during a fifteen year period, provided this militarily ambitious nation with the necessary expertise to expand its own naval shipbuilding industry.

Importantly, foreign orders helped to boost the revenue of the company during the lean inter-war period and again after 1945. Between 1918 and the outbreak of World War II, forty two warships and submarines were launched at Barrow for the Royal Navy and a further seventeen for other countries. Only thirteen RN vessels, all submarines, including four, tiny X-Craft, were constructed between 1945-59 but a further five, medium-sized surface warships were completed for two South American nations.

In the foreseeable future, it is likely that the small Israeli submarine **Rahav**, launched in May 1977 with no fanfare or acclaim owing to political sensitivities, will be the last in a long line of naval vessels to be built by Vickers on overseas contracts. The plain fact is that this firm, like most of its dwindling number of rivals across the UK, has been unable to remain competitive in the international shipbuilding market. It is beyond the remit of this book properly to explore the ramifications of the EC regulations that forbad a designated warship-building yard like Vickers from accessing monies from the Shipbuilding Intervention Fund in order to pursue mercantile orders that might have saved jobs in a town so dependent on its shipbuilding and engineering base. In the late 1980s, VSEL employed 14,000 workers; in six years it shed over 9,000 jobs.

Likewise, there is only space to make passing reference to the fact that Vickers, at the same time as it was building warships, was also constructing and outfitting a significantly large tonnage of merchant shipping of all kinds including several elegant liners. As an engineering firm, it designed and constructed the machinery, including the engines and boilers which drove the ships and submarines, while its reputation as an armaments' manufacturer is certainly not limited simply to naval guns.

In 2008, the future prospects for the Barrow workforce look reasonably secure within the notoriously unpredictable, interrelated world of shipbuilding, defence and politics. The 2006 White Paper on the future of the UK's Independent Strategic Nuclear Deterrent seemed to point the way for the Cumbrian firm to be involved in the construction of a future class of nuclear powered SSBNs at some stage during the next decade. However, although the announcement that the central 'blocks' for the aircraft carriers **HMS Queen Elizabeth** and **Prince of Wales** are to be constructed by the BAE section of the ACA Consortium, at the time of writing it is not entirely certain that the contract will be undertaken at Barrow.

The company that once was Vickers, Sons and Maxim Ltd. of Barrow-in-Furness is now a subsidiary of BAE Systems, a multi-national concern engaged in the development, delivery and support of a considerable range of advanced defence and aerospace systems. It is equally futile to bemoan this loss of a famous name as it is to speculate on what will happen in the next hundred years with respect to Barrow's most important employer. Perhaps it is sufficient at this point in its history simply to applaud the achievements of a dedicated workforce who, over several generations, has been responsible for so many fine ships and submarines that have served the Navy well.

Jon Wise
November 2008

3

A panoramic picture of Barrow looking south east across the town towards Morecambe Bay and the Lancashire coast. In the foreground is Vickerstown built for the company workers at the turn of the last century to solve an acute housing shortage. The docks visible in the middle distance are, from left to right, Devonshire, Buccleuch and Ramsden Dock with the large square expanse of Cavendish Dock beyond. Part of the Reserve Fleet can be seen berthed in trots on the southern side of Buccleuch Dock and there is also a large floating dock in Devonshire Dock. The entrance to the graving dock, to be seen at the far end of Devonshire and now no longer in use, was via the Walney Channel in the foreground which necessitated vessels being towed to and from their fitting out berths through the entire dock system.

(BAE Systems Submarine Solutions)

A rather wintry view of the town with the dark mass of buildings in the centre constituting the bulk of the Vickers works. The wide, straight Michaelson Road crosses the water dividing Devonshire Dock on the left and Buccleuch Dock on the right and leads on to Barrow town centre beyond. The two large hammerhead cranes used for shipping very heavy items of equipment can be seen alongside the fitting-out berths in the two docks. The slipways are in the foreground facing Walney Island across the channel. This photograph was taken in the 1950s when merchant ship production, particularly tankers, formed the bulk of the orders, as witnessed here. Vickers-Armstrongs, like other British shipbuilders, profited from the 'Long Boom' between 1945 and 1965, when the demand for merchant ships soared during a prolonged period of economic growth. The covered sheds in the left foreground, which appear to be in a semi-derelict state, were used for submarine building during WWII.

(BAE Systems Submarine Solutions)

This view of Devonshire Dock looking westwards was probably taken in 1896 the year before the Naval Construction and Armament Company became Vickers, Sons & Maxim Ltd. The vessel in the centre of the trio alongside the fitting-out berth is **HMS Powerful**, a four-funnelled, protected cruiser. Her construction marked an important milestone for a workforce that had only started building warships of any size some six years earlier. **HMS Powerful**, and her sister **Terrible** built at Clydebank were, in their day, the largest cruisers ever built. She had a displacement of 14,200 tons and was 538 feet in length. Her very large hull was required in order to accommodate novel triple expansion engines, 2,975 tons of bunkers plus a sizeable complement of stokers. Either side of **Powerful**, and dwarfed by her, are the 5,600 tons cruisers **Doris** and **Juno**. The large building on the other side of the dock is the Corn Mill, a prominent feature of the Barrow landscape for many years. *(Author's Collection)*

6

Large crowds on the water's edge witness the launch of **HMS Vengeance** on the 25th July 1899. *Vengeance* was the first battleship to be built by the new Vickers Sons & Maxim Ltd. and constituted the realisation of an ambition by Albert Vickers to produce a vessel "built, engined, armoured and supplied with her heavy gun-mountings" by his firm. The 12,900 tons pre-Dreadnought, seen here in her Victorian livery of black hull, white boot topping and superstructure, differed from her sister ships of the Canopus Class in being 'hard-ended'; this meant that, in addition to her side and bulkhead armour, she had thin armour plate fore and aft. Vickers had selected Krupp armour for the ship and, in the process, had produced a nickel chromium steel plate with a high carbon content which proved to be a very successful light-weight armour. It was subsequently used on the Cressy Class cruisers. *Vengeance* was actively employed during World War I in Africa and in the Mediterranean where she saw action during the Dardanelles Campaign.

(The Dock Museum Cat. No. 2367)

Holland submarine No. 2 at the extreme eastern end of Buccleuch Dock and about to pass under the railway bridge and into Ramsden Dock. It is likely that the boat was undergoing trials at the time this rather contrived photograph was taken in 1902. Vickers, Sons & Maxim Ltd. not only built all five of the Holland Class, they were also the Royal Navy's sole submarine contractor up until 1912. The design used for ***Holland 1*** was the Adder 10 design, as yet unbuilt in the USA. Vickers found many impracticalities in the design during build but could not make changes without invalidating the performance guarantee. Under the contract terms, Captain Frank Cable, the Holland trial captain with Electric Boat in the USA, was sent to Barrow to assist with trials. Only when ***Holland 1*** nearly turned turtle in the docks with Captain Cable aboard were Vickers approved to make whatever changes they deemed necessary. Vickers engineers became so adept at submarine design that they produced their own submarine design and had it accepted by the Admiralty.   Four were ordered initially. The first boat, ***A 1***, was completed in 1902, the same year as the Holland boats. A further nine A-Class were subsequently ordered and built. The last of these (***A 13***) was experimentally fitted with a diesel engine but diesel propulsion was not to be introduced generally until the D Class. The relationship between Vickers and Electric Boat was renewed in the late 50s in the period leading up to the build of ***Dreadnought*** and has been rekindled in the new Millennium on the Astute Programme. The building of these submarines was supposed to be secret but, owing to the elementary nature of security at the time, news had leaked out by March 1901. Built to a 'spindle hull' design, with all tanks and machinery inside the pressure hull, these submarines were extremely cramped for their crews.

(The Dock Museum Cat. No. 3441)

8

This photograph affords a good view of **HMS Holland 5** apparently about to be loaded aboard a coaster alongside. Her 'tear-drop' shaped hull presents a profile not dissimilar to the nuclear boats which were produced by the same yard more than half a century later. Note the single set of hydroplanes and the rudder aft. The lack of freeboard and conning tower made surface navigation both difficult and hazardous. However, Vickers did introduce a hinged periscope which was lacking in the equivalent American boats. Although the ambitious British firm was anxious to start designing its own submarines at the time and to sever ties with the Electric Boat Company this was not to be the case as the companies subsequently became financially linked. **Holland 5** had an undistinguished, short career, running aground at 'Promotion Point' off Fort Blockhouse in 1910 and foundering on her way to the breakers' yard two years later.

(Furness Newspapers)

The two figures in view give an impression of the vast dimensions of the naval gunshop, the output of which constituted a significant portion of the business of the Barrow works, particularly in the early years of the 20th Century. Only Elswick across the Pennines in Newcastle possessed a similar armament building capacity. The four 7.5-inch guns nearest the camera were destined to form part of the secondary armament of **HMS Shannon**, one of three Minotaur Class armoured cruisers built for the 1904 Programme. The cruiser itself was constructed at H.M. Naval Dockyard Chatham. The shape of the turrets in the background suggests that they might belong to the main armament; **Shannon** was fitted with four 9.2-inch guns in twin turrets sited fore and aft. The dockyard manager seen on the left is standing next to a 12 pdr. anti-torpedo gun, one of sixteen carried by these cruisers, which gives a measure of the perceived threat from this type of vessel at the time. *(The Dock Museum Cat. No. 6486)*

The Vickers staff have been carefully posed for this publicity photograph both to demonstrate the process of loading a handworked gun and for obvious dramatic effect. The shot is taken inside one of *Katori*'s 6-inch casemates and shows the charge about to be rammed home behind the shell. The gunlayer is on the left. This pre-Dreadnought and her close sister *HIJMS Kashima*, which was built by the rival firm Armstrong at Elswick, were the last Japanese battleships to be designed and built abroad. Vickers was also responsible for designing and constructing the guns, turrets and mountings for this 16,400 tons ship which was launched in August 1905. She lasted less than twenty years in the Imperial Japanese Navy; obsolete almost from the point of completion, she was scrapped in 1924 in order to conform to the Washington Naval Treaty of 1922.

(The Dock Museum Cat. No. 4242)

The strict security surrounding the building of **HMS D1** is noticeable in this seemingly deserted scene. Following her launch in May 1908, the submarine was towed to a remote wharf for completion, screened from view both on land and seaward sides. These measures are understandable in view of the fact that this boat incorporated important advances in submarine design. Her class were the first British boats to have external ballast tanks which provided far more space inside, their twin screws afforded greater manoeuvrability and the introduction of diesel engines that were not only more reliable tha petrol-fuelled engines but also brought an end to the noxious and dangerous petrol fumes which crews of earlier classes had to suffer. Finally, they were the first to be fitted with wireless telegraphy (W/T); an aerial was strung from the bridge (still to be fitted in this picture) to a bow stump mast.

(The Dock Museum Cat. No. 0113)

The Imperial Russian Navy armoured cruiser *Rurik* photographed at Toulon. Vickers had to win an international design competition in order to secure the contract for this ship although it is alleged that the firm had been courting the Russian Admiralty for some time through its chief agent, Basil Zaharoff. While the Russians quibbled over some of the finer points of the design, Vickers moved rapidly ahead with construction so that by the time the final contract was signed in January 1906, 2,600 tons of steel was already assembled on the slipway. *Rurik* was launched in November of that year and then transferred to William Beardmore and Co. at Dalmuir for fitting out including the installation of her substantial armour. Beardmore had become specialists in the manufacture of armour at the time; their new 12,000 ton hydraulic press was considered the best in the country. The firm welcomed the task as there was little other work at the yard at the time. The fact that Vickers had recently acquired a substantial shareholding in Beardmore and the latter owed them a good deal of money may also have had a bearing on the matter. *Rurik* joined the Russian fleet late in 1908.

(The Dock Museum Cat. No. 0322)

13

A spectacular view of *HIJMS Kongo* entering the water on the 18th May 1912 at the pinnacle of Vickers' reputation as a shipbuilder of international status. The Japanese had paid the firm to build a series of warships incorporating the latest technology in order to gain experience; *Kongo* was to be the last battlecruiser design to be prepared outside Japan and the last capital ship to be built abroad for that country. This 27,500 tons sister of *HMS Lion* cost £2,500,000 and was superior in capability to earlier British battlecruisers. There was a naval scandal in Japan in 1914 during which it was alleged that Admiral Fuji had taken bribes from a Vickers' employee in connection with the contract for *Kongo*. The ship itself was in active service until 1944 when she was torpedoed and sunk by an American submarine.

(The Dock Museum Cat. No. 3176)

14

HMS Princess Royal berthed in Buccleuch Dock in an advanced state of completion, whilst *HIJMS Kongo* outboard floats high in the water, indicating that very little had been added to her basic hull at this stage. The two handcarts in view along with the generally chaotic state of the quayside appear in marked contrast to the sleek and technologically advanced warships alongside. The large building in the background, glimpsed between the crane and *Princess Royal* , is the Airship Shed built over the water in Cavendish Dock. The photograph, taken in 1912, affords a good sight of the funnels and control top of the battlecruiser; a further £68,000 was added to her construction cost when it was found necessary to move the foremast forward and to raise the height of the second and third funnels. *(The Dock Museum Cat. No. 0333)*

The Vickers' trials crew, immediately recognisable in their suits and flat caps, can be seen on the decks of the 1,200 tons monitor *Javary* as she heads for the Clyde trials area. Most unusually, this vessel and her two sisters were constructed and launched sideways into Walney Channel. These shallow-draught gunboats had been designed by Vickers for Brazil before a crisis in rubber prices led to the country's economic collapse and the end of the deal. The monitors were subsequently laid up from February 1914 until the outbreak of war, whereupon they were purchased by the British Government for £155,000 each in order to prevent them from being sold to a potential enemy. *Javary* was re-named **HMS Humber**. She saw long and extensive service off Belgium, in the Dardanelles and elsewhere in the Middle East. In March 1919, she was refitted for deployment to North Russia. The monitor is proceeding independently in this photograph; owing to a low freeboard and very shallow draught, long passages had to be taken under tow with the ship closed down.

(Author's Collection)

HMS Revenge presents a magnificent and imposing sight on March 23rd 1916 as she steams at full speed on sea trials during which she officially achieved 21.9 knots. Admiral Charles Madden criticised **Revenge** for being very wet in a seaway with "a continual cloud of spray forward". This is not apparent on what is evidently a fine and fairly calm day in the Clyde. Although only ten months elapsed between launch and completion, Vickers was not unduly burdened at the time with the construction of large tonnage ships and was concentrating instead on its considerable submarine workload. The reduced size of the Royal Sovereign Class battleships, in comparison with the earlier Queen Elizabeth Class, made them cramped amidships and therefore unsuitable for large-scale modernization later in their careers.

(The Dock Museum Cat. No. 2089)

HMS V3 was one result of the findings of a 1912 Committee which looked at future requirements for coastal submarines. **V3**, the letter denoted that it is a Vickers' design, had a submerged displacement of 486 tons. They were partially double-hulled, the outer hull being faired into the pressure hull fore and aft. Vickers claimed that the submarines could dive to 150 feet, giving them a superiority in this respect over contemporary boats. This was due to the extra strength provided by external framing between the inner and outer hull. Experience during WW1 showed that, although the design met requirements, there was little employment for these small submarines and only four were built. **V3**, which was launched in April 1915, was sold for scrap just five years later. She is seen here in Devonshire Dock under her own power with the Iron and Steel Works in the background.

(The Dock Museum Cat. No. 0001)

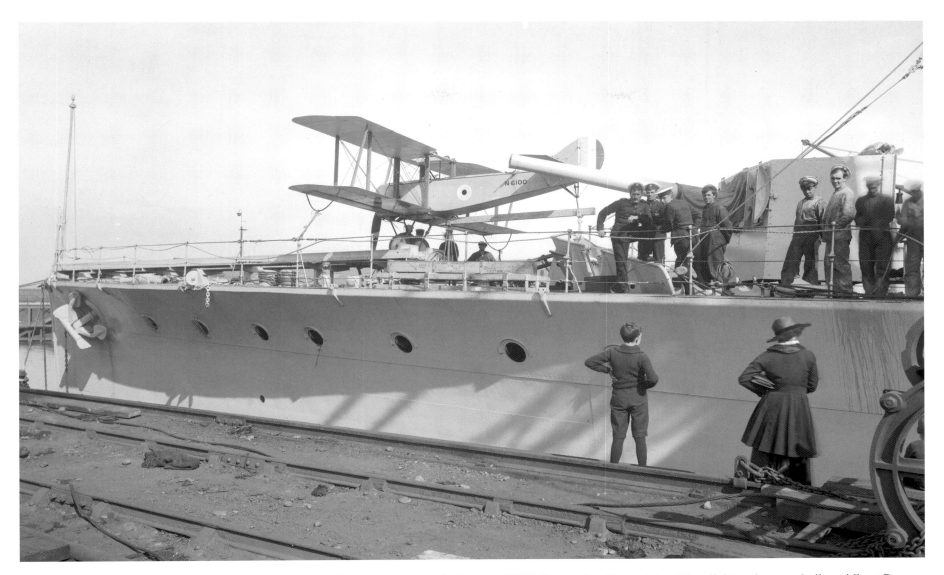

The first production Beardmore WBIII aircraft on her launch ramp fitted over the bows of *HMS Cassandra*. The Caledon Class light cruiser was built rapidly at Barrow as part of the WW1 Emergency War Programme; only fifteen months elapsed between laying down and completion in June 1917. Out of sight in this photograph is the small aircraft hanger fitted alongside the bridge superstructure on the starboard side. The ship appears complete; the informal scene captured in this photograph suggests that the ship is shortly to depart. *Cassandra* was lost when she encountered an uncharted German minefield in the Baltic during operations against the Bolsheviks in December 1918.

(The Dock Museum Cat. No. 348)

The head foreman, complete with trilby hat, inspects the stern launch cradle beneath the immaculately painted hull of the 14,650 tons submarine depot ship *Medway* while shipwrights put the finishing touches to the heavily greased sliding ways. The ship was designed to support the overseas patrol submarines of the O and P Classes. Vickers seriously underestimated *Medway*'s topweight and it was found that, at deep load, her metacentric height exceeded thirteen feet. An excessive metacentric height is considered undesirable as it causes a ship to roll quite violently, although it does not make her liable to capsize. On one occasion, she rolled 42 degrees each way with a period of nine seconds between each roll during which she lost her main mast. Nevertheless this diesel-engined ship was popular with submariners: she was considered comfortable, easy to work in and accommodating. A primary reason for this was that *Medway*, launched in 1927, had been purpose-built and was not a hasty wartime conversion.

(The Dock Museum Cat. No. 3995)

Vickers were responsible for four of the six Parthian Class Overseas Patrol submarines built during the period 1928-31 and originally earmarked for service on the China Station. **HMS Proteus** is seen here on a bright day in July 1929. It is interesting to note the cloth-capped uniformity of a smartly turned-out launch crew. These boats differed externally from the slightly earlier Odin Class by virtue of a streamlined bow and the platform for the 4-inch gun which has yet to be fitted in its position forward of **Proteus**' fin. Stiffening has been added to the external fuel tanks near the bow and she is lacking her forward hydroplanes at this stage. **Proteus** survived WWII before being scrapped in 1946.

(Steve Bush Collection)

HMS Resource in 1929, accompanied by no fewer than four tugs, being towed well clear of land before commencing her builder's trials. She has already received her 'tropical' colour scheme ready for service on the China Station. The 12,300 tons fleet repair ship shared similar underwater and deck protection to the slightly larger submarine depot ship **Medway** also built at Barrow in the late twenties. Internal bilges, similar to those in the battleship **HMS Nelson**, were fitted, she had a 1$\frac{1}{2}$-inch torpedo bulkhead amidships for protection against torpedo attack and 1$\frac{1}{2}$-inch deck armour. Four 4-inch, 45 calibre QF guns comprised what was considered at the time to be a powerful anti-aircraft armament. **Resource** survived the war before being scrapped in 1954.

(The Dock Museum Cat. No. 2093)

HMS Perseus alongside in April 1930 following completion. The large, well-dressed group posing for this photograph include naval officers and shipyard managers. The bowler-hatted gentleman (tenth from the left in the back row) is Charles Craven, Managing Director and later Chairman of Vickers-Armstrongs Ltd, an influential and colourful figure in the company's history. At this stage the submarine is fitted with a 4.7in./40 QF Mk. X gun which she carried until 1933 when, in common with other boats of the class, it was replaced with the 4-in. Mk.IV. *Perseus* sank in 270 feet of water after striking an Italian mine off the Greek coast in December 1941. Remarkably, one survivor managed to escape and swim to the surface fortified by a "stiff livener of rum."

(*The Dock Museum Cat. No. 0003*)

In the centre of the photograph, a gang of riveters is at work on the pressure hull of the first **HMS Porpoise**. The portable forge, where the rivets were heated, is to the left of the group. Another gang, undertaking similar tasks, is visible in the background. The fact that some of the men are in shirtsleeves suggests that the weather is mild but this image illustrates, nonetheless, the lack of shelter for the workers on the slipway where the boat would have been constructed from keel upwards. This photograph was taken in 1932, the year of her launch.

(The Dock Museum Cat. No. 0012)

A Vickers-built twin-mounted 4-inch Mk.N 45-calibre gun aboard the Brazilian Sail Training Ship *Almirante Saldanha* which was probably occupying the Barrow Floating Dock at the time this view was taken in 1934. She was launched in December 1933, became a survey ship in 1958 and was not disposed of until 1990. In addition to the 4-inch guns, this four-masted barquentine was also equipped with a 3-inch A.A. gun, four 3-pounders, a 13mm A.A., two machine guns and one 21-inch torpedo tube. Although her declared task was midshipman training, she clearly had the capability to work with seaman specialists as well. Vickers-Armstrongs was also responsible for the auxiliary diesel engine which was a four-cycle, single acting, airless injection, trunk piston reversible diesel. This developed 1,400bhp when running at 90 rpm providing a speed of 11 knots.

(The Dock Museum Cat. No. 0481)

The Portuguese submarines **Delfim**, **Espadarte** and **Golfino** together on the slipway, probably in early 1934. **Delfim**, on the left, is the most advanced in construction and she appears to have received her final coat of paint ahead of her launch on 1st May. The framework for the canopy, which traditionally shelters the launch party, can be seen at the bottom left of the picture. There is activity aft of her fin where a riveter's hearth on the casing suggests work is in progress on finishing her hull. To her left, **Espadarte** and **Golfino** both to be launched on the same day, 30 May 1934, are at a similar stage. The supporting ribs of the hull casing are exposed together with the circular casements for the 4-in guns. These 1,092 tons medium-sized patrol submarines designed by Vickers were smaller than contemporary British boats although similar in design and appearance.

(The Dock Museum Cat. No. 0035)

Naval personnel and members of the trials party can be seen engaged in conversation on the forward casing and around the gun of **HMS Severn**, the second of three Thames (or River) Class submarines all built by Vickers-Armstrongs at Barrow in the period 1931-35. The boat was on sea trials and was at anchor when this photograph was taken in 1935. The Thames Class were intended to combine the roles of fleet and patrol submarine but critics of the design maintained that they were too slow to operate with the latest battleships while their large size made them cumbersome to manoeuvre underwater. They cost over £500,000 each to build which largely explains why the original projection for twenty boats never materialized.

(The Dock Museum Cat. No. 0016)

A crowded fitting-out berth in the submarine dock area in early 1935. The boat alongside, and nearest the camera, is *HMS Severn*. Ahead of her, with her bows out, is the Portuguese *Delfim*. *Severn's* sister *Clyde* completes this trio. A second Portuguese boat, *Golfino*, lies alongside the floating dock which is here occupied by her sister *Espadarte*. The scaffolding and staging indicate that there is a good deal of activity taking place on the latter two Portuguese boats and also on *HMS Clyde* which was approximately two months behind her Thames Class sister. The Low Level Bridge can be seen at the far end of Devonshire Dock and beyond it the exit lock into Walney Channel. The Graving Dock can be made out to the right of the lock beside the crane.

(The Dock Museum Cat. No. 0314)

The Leander Class cruiser **HMS Ajax** at the fitting out berth in Devonshire Dock in June 1935 with the destroyers **HMS Fame** and **Firedrake** alongside. The bows of the passenger ship **Orion** are visible in the background beyond the High Level Bridge. All three warships are complete and it appears that **Ajax** is receiving her final coat of paint. During the first half of the decade, naval contracts were scarce but the differential in the wage bill between naval and merchant ship construction remained considerable, owing to the large numbers of skilled workers required to build a warship. It was estimated at the time that the labour bill for an 8,000-ton cruiser was equal to that of about twenty similar-sized cargo ships. Electric arc welding was used quite extensively on the Leander Class as the Admiralty sought to encourage this comparatively new shipbuilding technique in the face of stiff resistance from, amongst others, the Boilermakers' Union. **Firedrake** was torpedoed and sunk in the North Atlantic in December 1942 but her sister ship survived the war and was transferred to the Dominican Navy in 1948. **HMS Ajax** gave distinguished service during which she gained nine battle honours.

(The Dock Museum Cat. No. 388)

ARA Entre Ríos was one of three Vickers-built Buenos Aires Class destroyers all of which were launched for Argentina on the same day, 21st September 1937. Contracts for the remaining four ships of the class were also awarded to British shipyards. They were constructed to a modified Royal Navy G Class design as this photograph of ***Entre Ríos*** undergoing sea trials clearly demonstrates. Argentina possessed the most powerful South American navy during the first half of the 20th Century and in 1926 embarked on an expensive and ambitious ten-year modernisation plan to maintain this superiority. The training ship ***La Argentina***, a modified Arethusa Class cruiser, which was launched at Barrow six months earlier than the destroyers, was part of this programme. ***Entre Ríos*** remained in service until 1973.

(The Dock Museum Cat. No. 0586)

A Vickers employee has been invited to pose for this photograph in order to give an indication of scale. The notice behind his head is self-explanatory; 732 is the Yard Number awarded to **HMS Illustrious**, the name ship and first of class. The carrier was fitted with three sets of these Parsons geared turbines which in turn served the triple screw installation. However, this was not an entirely satisfactory arrangement and vibration was felt in the island superstructure while the ship was on trials. Although not considered serious at the time, was to become acute by the end of the war. **Illustrious'** machinery produced 113,700 shp and 234.2 rpm on trials in May 1940 giving a speed of 30 knots.

(The Dock Museum Cat. No. 2898)

This unusual viewpoint from the top of a crane shows *HMS Ursula* gathering sternway as she ploughs into Walney Channel following her launch on 16th February 1938. Tension was rising across Europe at the time; Austria was about to be annexed and the Munich Crisis was just over six months away. The fact that no fewer than three Royal Navy submarines were launched at Barrow on the same day was no doubt orchestrated to send a clear message to the German Government. The others were *Ursula*'s sister *Unity* and the T Class *HMS Triumph*. *Ursula*, along with *Unity* and *Undine*, belonged to the first group of their class and differed from all but one of the later boats due to the prominent bulbous bow casing containing their external torpedo tubes. The U Class as designed were intended as unarmed training submarines but urgent operational requirements for smaller submarines to operate in the Mediterranean prompted the need to 'shoehorn' torpedo tubes into the submarines already ordered and in build. Later U Class benefited from the opportunity to allow for tubes etc in the redesign. *(Steve Bush Collection)*

It is quite likely that the employees waving their caps, while standing rather unsafely on what appears to be sheet metal, have been instructed to appear in this way for the purpose of this press photograph which was intended for world-wide distribution. Intentionally or not, the furled Union Jack and the two managers standing proudly on the fin complete a perfectly constructed message about rearmament and defiance in the face of German expansionism. This is the launch of **HMS Triumph** on 16th February 1938. The 53 boats of the T Class made them the largest class of ocean-going submarines built for the RN. Barrow constructed no fewer than 28 which at the time put a considerable strain on the workforce. This was in marked contrast to the depression years of the early 1930s when the yard was desperately short of contracts. *(Steve Bush Collection)*

33

Crowds line the shore on the 4th April 1939 as **HMS Illustrious** takes to the water for the first time. The nameship of her class, **Illustrious** was also the first aircraft carrier to be built by Vickers. Five of the Rea Company tugs are preparing to tow the ship from the Walney Channel, through the Ramsden Dock lock to her fitting-out berth in Buccleuch Dock. A considerable amount of timber shoring from the launch together with parts of the white painted cradle are to be seen in the water. Interestingly, unlike later carriers to be built at the yard, both **Illustrious** and **Indomitable** launched the following year lacked their island superstructure at this stage.

(The Dock Museum Cat. No. 2404)

The completed carrier **HMS Illustrious** passing the lifeboat station on Roa Island with Piel Island in the distance. She is probably under tow by the tugs **Calgarth** and **Langarth** at this stage because this stretch of water would have provided insufficient steerage for such a large vessel to proceed independently. This photograph is dated 1939, therefore several months before her final departure from Barrow on 20th April 1940 when she accidentally sank the tug **Poolgarth**. Her delivery date had been postponed because of delays in fitting her radar. The tender for **HMS Illustrious** was for the hull to cost £1,690,000 and the machinery, also to be built at Barrow, to amount to £705,000.

(The Dock Museum Cat. No. 0623)

HMS Urchin heading up the Walney Channel towards the dock gates. The shipyard cranes can be seen in the right background and beyond the shadowy shape of Black Combe behind the town. *Urchin* was one of two U-Class destroyers built at Barrow; she was completed in September 1943 which probably dates this photograph as she is in the process of completing her sea trials. *Urchin* was one of forty U - CA Classes of destroyer ordered under the 1941 New Construction Programme. It is a measure of the pressure on UK shipyards at the time, with respect to the very high demand for fleet destroyers, that this was considered to be the maximum number that could be laid down during the war. After a period in reserve post war, *Urchin* was converted into a Type 15 anti-submarine frigate. *(The Dock Museum Cat. No. 0697)*

HMS Spartan's camouflage paint, probably dark grey, light blue and pale grey, is effective against the dark background of the shipyard workshops. She is in the latter stages of fitting out in Buccleuch Dock. *Spartan* belonged to the Bellona Sub Group which were four turret versions of the Dido Class cruisers, but carried a quite different profile with lowered bridge and no rake to funnels or masts. Laid down in December 1939 as part of the New Construction War Programme, *Spartan* did not complete until August 1943. Work on this programme was suspended following Dunkirk, firstly so that earlier warship orders that were urgently needed could be accelerated and, secondly, to reduce the requirements for materials. In the case of the Bellona Sub Group, there was a shortage of 5.25-inch guns. This suspension led to the redesign referred to above that was made in light of wartime experience.

(The Dock Museum Cat. No. 0671)

Vickers built six of the twelve XE Class midget submarines to be constructed, collectively Yard No.939, during the period December 1943 to January 1945. This series of boats were improvements on the previous X Class, some of which saw action during Operation Source, the daring raid on the battleship *Tirpitz* in 1943. They featured air-conditioning, spring-loaded legs for landing on the seabed, an air-lock for use by the boat's diver and extra stowage space. The Barrow XE boats later formed the 14th Submarine Flotilla which was sent to the Far East where *XE-3* became famous for its attack on the Japanese heavy cruiser *Takao* in the Jahore Strait. This carefully composed photograph shows one of the boats undergoing basin trials in Devonshire Dock with storage tanks and the Corn Mill in the background.

(The Dock Museum Cat. No. 0139)

Two naval personnel are, somewhat casually, using the support bar for balance as the completed midget submarine **XT5** is lowered by crane onto the quayside next to Devonshire Dock. The operation is being watched carefully by a head foreman on the right of the picture. The XT craft were built for training purposes, particularly to free up submarines that had been employed as anti-submarine targets. Vickers delivered six of these boats by March 1944 and they were subsequently employed at **HMS Seahawk** on Loch Fyne. The XT craft differed substantially from the operational boats, lacking cargo release gear and having a fixed induction mast.

(The Dock Museum Cat. No. 0142)

This photograph, probably dating from 1944, shows the Assembly Shop full of prefabricated sections for A-Class submarines, some awaiting transfer to the building slips, others in various stages of construction. The aft-end section to be seen in the left foreground belongs to **HMS Amphion** (ex-**Anchorite**) which was to be completed in March 1945, one of only two A-Class to be commissioned before the end of the war. Her Yard Number 910 is clearly visible along with other marks made by the 'liners-off' who supplied the essential information for the shipwrights, platers and others to work on the vessel. Two midships sections are to be seen in the background together with a bow section which is awaiting plating.

(The Dock Museum Cat. No. 0218)

A significant advance in shipbuilding technique is evident in this view of the A-Class submarine **HMS Alliance** in 1944. Large sections of the boat's pressure hull have been constructed in the workshops under cover before being brought to the slipway to be joined together. Electric welding has been employed, to the complete exclusion of riveting, throughout the hull, external tanks and casing. The cylindrical profile of the amidships sections and the conical shaped bow length are clearly visible here. In order to achieve diving depths of 500 feet, strict circularity of the hull was essential. Welding helped achieve the desired streamlined shape as well as offering consider-able savings in weight and space when compared with riveting.

(The Dock Museum Cat. No. 0223)

Landing Ship Tank (LST) 3007, seen here under tow, was originally to have been built by Harland and Wolff but the order was moved to Vickers for completion along with ***LST 3006***. Both formed part of the 1944 Programme and were finished at Barrow along with two other LST(3)s. ***LST 3007*** was launched in September 1944 and completed the following May. Originally, these landing ships were to be repeats of the LST(2) type but a re-think became necessary owing to the unavailability of the locomotive type diesels used previously as a means of propulsion. The comparative lack of welding facilities in British yards at the time was also a contributory factor in the eventual re-design of the vessels, despite the best efforts of the Admiralty and the Shipyard Development Committee during the war to change traditional practices and to move away from riveting as the accepted method of construction.

(The Dock Museum Cat. No. 0760)

It is a reflection of the company's involvement in other shipbuilding commitments during World War II, particularly submarines, that Vickers at Barrow was only responsible for building four of the 86 Hunt Class Escort Destroyers. It was a huge wartime undertaking, demanding heavy involvement from most of the other major UK warship builders. This is the Hunt Type III **HMS Catterick** which, along with **Derwent**, **Penylan** and **Rockwood**, were ordered as part of the 1940 Building Programme. *Catterick* was laid down in March 1941 and completed fifteen months later. She was the only one of the four to survive the war, being transferred to Greece in 1946. *Catterick* is seen here underway in Walney Channel proceeding at seven knots.

(The Dock Museum Cat. No. 0676)

A large midships section of the pressure hull of **HMS Alcide** being transported to the top yard by the hauliers Edward Box and Co. Ltd, on the 2nd January 1945. The advantage of prefabrication is illustrated here as this A-Class boat was to be launched less than fourteen weeks later. Thus time working on the submarine in the open during the late winter months would be reduced to a minimum. This boat was officially laid down exactly a month after this photograph was taken. Buccleuch Dock is in the background, Barrow town centre is on the other side of the water with the Town hall, a prominent landmark, on the left. *(The Dock Museum Cat. No. 2005)*

The Venezuelan destroyer **FNV Zulia** in the early stages of construction on the 25th November 1951. The main after transverse bulkhead and a section of the keel are in place. The location numbers on the bottom cross-beams can just be made out. She had been laid down four months earlier, the same day as her sistership **FNV Nueva Esparta** which can be seen on the adjoining berth. It would be a further two years before this ship was launched. Pre-war, this stage in a ship's construction, when there was no form of shelter from the vessel, was a particularly uncertain time for the Barrow shipwrights. If it rained or snowed and there were no dry jobs, they were sent home with 'white pass-outs' which meant no pay. This practice was re-introduced after the war but representations by the Shipwrights' Union soon led to its abandonment.

(The Dock Museum Cat. No. 2220)

Managers and head foremen watch proceedings intently as 'A' gun is carefully lowered into position on board the Venezuelan destroyer *FNV Nueva Esparta* in Devonshire Dock in 1953. Another of the British designed twin Mk IV 4.5-inch gun mountings can be seen on the quayside. Vickers-Armstrongs had offered the design of this large destroyer to the Venezuelan Government, together with one for a medium-sized destroyer, in 1949. The order for this ship and her sister *Zulia*, confirmed the following year, was worth £5,000,000. This came at an important time amidst the austerity of the early 1950s when Vickers was anxious to re-establish its fruitful, pre-war links with foreign navies. The Venezuelan Government also contemplated placing an order for a small cruiser at the time but this came to nothing. However, a third of this class, *FNV Aragua*, was later also built at the Barrow, the trio becoming the major units of this South American Navy over the next two decades.

(The Dock Museum Cat. No. 0717)

46

The large, prefabricated after section of the hull of **HMS Explorer** is being manoeuvred out of the assembly shed on its way to the slipway, probably in late 1953. The boat's propellers have yet to be fitted but the prominent stabiliser fins forward of the rudder are in place. The High Test Peroxide (HTP) was stored in rubberised canvas bags located under the casing in the free flood space, the sea water pressure causing the fuel in the bags to be released on demand and acting to compensate for the fuel used. **Explorer** was launched in March 1954 but it was to be two further years before she commenced her first of class trials. *(The Dock Museum Cat. No. 2031)*

The smartly-painted aft 4.5in gun mounting stands out in stark contrast to the rust-streaked appearance of the rest of *FNV Nueva Esparta*, name-ship of the class of 2,600 tons destroyers built for the Venezuelan Navy. She is in the latter stages of fitting out in 1953 and is in the Graving Dock at the western end of the Vickers complex. This dock is no longer in use and the town's Dock Museum has been built over one end. *Nueva Esparta* was equipped with both depth charge throwers and racks and these can be seen on the quarter-deck. Her sistership *Zulia* returned to Barrow in 1959 to have Squid ASW mortars fitted in place of her torpedo tubes; this ship was similarly equipped at Palmer's, Hebburn.

(The Dock Museum Cat. No. 0709)

FNV Nueva Esparta departing Barrow for the last time on the 9th September 1954, some nine months after she had been completed. Superficially reminiscent of the RN's Battle Class, with the same turrets and raked funnel, in fact they were closer in size and layout to the Daring Class. However, a less efficient powerplant made for a shorter range than for a Daring and although the bridge design was considered superior to the British ship and the accommodation more expansive (at least for the officers), the ship had inferior radar and carried less ammunition and stores. In 1958 the ship was involved in a Venezuelan military coup and four years later ***Nueva Esparta*** formed part of Task Force 137 which undertook blockade duties during the Cuban missile crisis of 1962. She was refitted in the UK in 1958 and again a decade later when two Sea Cat SAM replaced twelve of her 40mm guns. The destroyer was disposed of in 1978.

(Ken Royall)

A wooden 'mock-up' of the motor room of **HMS Porpoise**. This photograph was most likely taken in the Joiners Shop where it would have been built. Traditionally, mock-ups of this kind were considered necessary especially in the construction of a first-of-class, in order to make sure that each piece of equipment fitted and to allow, hopefully, only minor adjustments to be made. What appeared possible on paper did not always translate satisfactorily to the cramped confines of a ship and particularly, as in this case, of a submarine. Critics of this form of full-scale simulation pointed out that altering or moving a large component made of wood was nearly as awkward and disruptive as shifting the real thing. In the end, sophisticated scale models and computer technology rendered this process obsolete. The downside would have been the effect on employment. In the late 1950s, for example, Vickers employed some 300 joiners.

(The Dock Museum Cat. No. 3591)

This photograph, dating from about 1954, shows a large midships section of **HMS Porpoise** being secured to a gantry for onward movement to the slipway. This portion of the pressure hull and part of the lower casing would have been constructed, probably in at least two parts, in the New Assembly Shop and would be joined to the fore and aft prefabricated sections over the next few months. A combination of clean, welded hulls and high underwater speeds contributed to the enviable reputation these boats were to enjoy. Vickers-Armstrongs built three of the eight Second Porpoise Class at Barrow and the name-ship was destined to become the first post-war operational submarine to be accepted into service. She was launched in April 1956.

(The Dock Museum Cat. No. 2065)

Heavy tarpaulins protect the midget submarine **HMS Stickleback** (X51) as she is transported on a low loader within the shipyard. Although the four boats of the class (X51-X54) were officially earmarked for harbour penetration trials and training, the true intention, spelt out in a 1955 Staff Requirement, was to equip them with nuclear mines which would be laid at the entrances to Soviet naval bases. The plan proved impracticable and effectively spelt the end of the Royal Navy's employment of midget submarines. The four X-Craft of this class were all built at Barrow under conditions of strict secrecy. *(The Dock Museum Cat. No. 0165)*

Majestic, the name-ship of the Majestic Class undergoing inclining tests in Buccleuch Dock in about August 1955. She was commissioned into the Australian Navy and renamed **HMAS Melbourne** on the 28th October 1955 over twelve years after she had been laid down. Following her launch in February 1945 work on her had been brought virtually to a standstill and was not resumed until 1949 when she was purchased by the Australian Government. Unlike her sistership **Sydney**, which was handed over in 1948, **Melbourne** benefited from several post-war British carrier innovations including angled flight deck, steam catapult, mirror deck landing sights plus a greatly enhanced radar suite which included three Type 277Q height finding sets.

(The Dock Museum Cat. No. 0687-03)

Increasing recognition of the advantages of constructing under cover is illustrated by this image of **HMS Rorqual** taken in the mid 1950s. Whereas each prefabricated section of the preceding A-Class submarines had been joined together on the slipway, here at least four lengths of the aft part of this Porpoise Class boat have already been welded together in the assembly shop prior to being moved outside for transportation to the slipway. Note the turntable in the right foreground. The Walney Channel can be seen on the left; the prominent white building in the background is the King Alfred Pub on Walney Island.

(The Dock Museum Cat. No. 2078)

The last of the three Venezuelan destroyers of the Nueva Esparta Class, **FNV Aragua**, returning to Barrow following gunnery trials in December 1955. These destroyers were specifically designed for service in the tropics, being both roomy and air-conditioned throughout. High freeboards helped their reputation as good seaboats in the often stormy tropical waters in which they operated. In common with other major naval units, **Aragua** was involved in a successful, navy-led coup in Venezuela in January 1958 which led to the overthrow of the President. She was the first of her class to be discarded in 1975 after less than 20 years' service. The massed cranes on the Vickers slipways can be seen in the background.

(Ken Royall)

HMS Explorer in Morecambe Bay using her HTP machinery during her Phase 2 Surface Proving Trials in late March 1956; the process referred to as 'fizzing' resulted in the clouds of pearly-grey exhaust gases. **Explorer** and her sister **Excalibur** were considered to be poor sea boats, their low fin making them uncomfortably wet during surface navigation. The experimental machinery proved so temperamental and difficult to handle during a nine-month trials period that in late June it was decided to abandon the programme temporarily to allow **Explorer** to be independently detached to work up "in slow time". This photograph was taken from **RFA Spabeck** which was employed as the submarine's HTP fuel carrier during the trials period.

(The Dock Museum Cat. No. 2058)

The funnel casing of the Whitby Class frigate *HMS Eastbourne* being lowered into position. The cylindrical shape of the original design for the class was intended to resist a nuclear blast. It proved both impractical and aesthetically unpopular and was soon replaced by the more familiar raked and domed version. The hull of the ship was built on the Tyne and had been towed to Barrow for completion. On arrival, it was found that there was a shortage of plans. It is alleged that this was remedied in the short term courtesy of the 'Eagle' Comic which had recently printed a general arrangement plan of the new class plus sectional drawings showing fitments, accommodation and weapons. When this photo was taken, probably in 1957, the foremast had yet to be fitted.
(*The Dock Museum Cat. No. 0747*)

This view of **HMS Eastbourne** being towed to the Graving Dock in mid-June 1957 shows the sharp V-form of the hull forward. The Type 12 frigates were built to operate at the 27-knots needed to counter contemporary submarines capable of 17-18 knots. As a result of this highly successful design these ships were able to avoid the usual problems when driving into heavy seas at speed. Still some considerable way short of completion, it is interesting to note that **Eastbourne** 's twin Mk10 ASW Limbo launchers have been shipped already. More successfully hidden beneath tarpaulin covers amidships are the torpedo tubes for the 21-inch Mk.20(E) ASW torpedoes which were destined never to become operational. Although some work appears to have been undertaken on the mounting, the twin 40mm STAAG gun, which covered the stern arcs, has yet to be fitted.

(Ken Royall)

Workers on board **HMS Porpoise** relax on the casing as the submarine is towed back to her fitting out berth on 14th June 1957 by two Furness Harbour tugs from the Graving Dock adjacent to Devonshire Dock. The nameship of her class, **Porpoise** was to complete the following April. Note the way that the struts supporting the temporary platform built over the buoyancy tanks have been shaped to match the curve of the hull. The missing part of the casing aft is above the diesel exhaust; this tended to be the last section to be completed on these submarines. Boats of this class were fitted with two Admiralty Standard Range 16-cylinder diesel generator sets which in turn supplied 3,300 bhp in order to provide a surface speed of 12 knots.

(Ken Royall)

Vickers built three out of the eight Second Porpoise Class submarines during the latter half of the 1950s. This is **Narwhal** which was launched on the 25th October 1957 and completed in May 1959. An important factor contributing to the success of this class and the follow-on Oberons was that their design benefited from experience and lessons learned over the past decade. This included analyses of wartime operations, examination of captured German U-boats and experiments with T-Class conversions. Porpoise Class submarines were designed with long patrol endurance in mind, their snort equipment being sufficiently advanced to cope with conditions worldwide and their habitability standards reflecting the move away from wartime austerity. Their large battery capacity could produce 880 volts for short bursts of underwater speed up to 17 knots. **Narwhal** gave 24 years' service before being sunk as a target in 1983.

(Ken Royall)

A gang of slingers positioning the very large Type 984 radar scanner with its fourteen foot diameter lens antenna, in the hold of a coaster, for onward movement to the carrier *Hermes* fitting out in Buccleuch Dock in 1958. At the time it was reckoned that this very complex three-dimensional radar, which fed a 32-track (Comprehensive Display System), should enable the fighter control officers to deal with twenty four contacts per minute. Type 984 was also fitted to *Victorious* and *Eagle*. The three warships in the background were part of the Reserve Fleet berthed at Barrow during the 1950s. They are, from the left, two River Class frigates, *Ballinderry* and *Exe*, and the Loch Class **HMS Loch Gorm**.

(The Dock Museum Cat. No. 2148)

Temporary lighting is burning brightly around the superstructure of the Chilean destroyer **Almirante Williams** which is lying alongside her fitting out berth on what is clearly a dismal Barrow day. Although her superstructure and the tubular foremast have been fitted, she lacks any of her armament and sensors suggesting that she is at a comparatively early stage of completion. Her heavily rust-stained hull is in stark contrast with the boot-topping and red-lead paint on the ship's bottom which would have been applied prior to launch. In order to achieve the precise lines evident in this photograph, shipwright liners-off would have marked the exact reference points, or 'pop-marks', on the ship's hull for the red leaders and painters to follow.

(Ken Royall)

A boiler being hoisted into position aboard *Almirante Williams* during her fitting out in Devonshire Dock. The prominent building in the background is the Corn Mill while the railway sheds can also be seen on the left. The destroyer was launched in May 1958 which would suggest that this photograph was probably taken later the same year. The Almirante Class were fitted with two Babcock and Wilcox boilers and two Vickers-built Parsons geared turbines constructed to a Parmetrada design; 54,000bhp provided a speed of 34.5 knots. A cruising speed of 16 knots gave the destroyers the range of 6,000 nautical miles which was necessary in order to cover adequately Chile's 4,000 mile coastline.

(The Dock Museum Cat. No. 2287)

Almirante Riveros, the second of the two destroyers built for the Chilean Government in the 1950s entering the choppy waters of Walney Channel on what was a wet and blustery day in December 1958. Initial negotiations for the two ships had been completed by November 1953 and the order was announced at Chilean Naval Headquarters in January 1954. It was confirmed nearly eighteen months later that they were to be built at Barrow to a modified UK Daring Class hull design with Battle Class destroyer internal arrangements. The fact that the Royal Naval Mission to Chile had re-established traditional naval links between the two countries in the immediate post-war period no doubt played a part in the decision to have the warships built in Britain. Vickers at Barrow had also been responsible for the successful build and delivery of three Capitan O'Brien Class submarines and their 9,000 tons depot ship ***Araucano*** in the late 1920s.

(Ken Royall)

The Buccleuch Dock fitting out berth was used to complete large ships such as **HMS Hermes** seen here on the 30th January 1959. Here she is nine months away from the start of her trials and the mass of scaffolding surrounding her island suggests that there is much work still to be finished. The tarpaulin covers on her forward flight-deck are apparently protecting the recesses for the 151ft. long BS4 steam catapults from the elements. A design outcome of the decision to fit the catapults which would enable **Hermes** to launch the latest jet aircraft was that the forward centre-line lift had to be moved to the deck edge. Unfortunately, when she was commissioned in November 1959, she could only operate twenty Sea Vixen, Scimitar and Buccaneer plus eight Gannet ASW aircraft because her small size meant that she couldn't accommodate the F4-K Phantom.

(Ken Royall)

65

The handsome lines of the completed Chilean destroyer *Almirante Williams*, characterisied by her raked funnels and mast, are evident in this photograph of her taken on the 6th September 1959. She has just exited the Graving Dock. Note the ladders and staging visible at various places on her superstructure. The ship, the first of the pair to reach this stage, commenced builder's trials during the course of the next few days ahead of her completion in March 1960. Her sistership followed nine months later. *Almirante Williams'* torpedo tubes, which were replaced by Exocet launchers during her 1971-2 refit, can be seen forward of her aft superstructure. In 1965, the Chilean Government commenced negotiations for the construction of two more destroyers. It is thought that these talks led eventually to the purchase of two Leander Class frigates, but these were built BY Yarrow on the Clyde and not at Barrow.

(Ken Royall)

The Oberon Class submarine **HMS Orpheus** photographed on her launch day in November 1959 with **HMS Dreadnought** under construction on the adjacent building berth. An aft section of the nuclear boat is already in place on the slipway. The temporary struts and crossbeams, used to support scaffolding and to maintain the circularity of the unit until decks and other equipment had been welded into position, are clearly visible inside all three hull units. The giant u-shaped cover encircling the rearmost section in this view suggests that welding work is taking place in this part of the submarine. Large piles of timber filling pieces and wedges used to prepare a ship for launch are stacked at the base of the crane. Despite being laid down some seventeen months after the nameship of her class, *Orpheus* was the first Oberon to be completed. This was probably due to the efficiency and experience in submarine construction of the large Barrow workforce. *Orpheus* had an aluminium superstructure whilst later boats adopted glass fibre laminate.

(Ken Royall)

Moving a large ship through the dock system at Barrow required deft handling. This was certainly the case when **HMS Hermes** left for the first time on trials. It was thought that the overhang from her angled flight deck would mean that there was very little clearance as she passed through the cradle or railway bridge separating Ramsden from Buccleuch Dock. Normally ships were eased through these narrow points with the aid of rafts of wooden fenders which kept the hull away from the coping stones of the dock wall. In the case of **Hermes**, the concern was that she would damage the raised railway bridge or vice versa. An elaborate system was devised involving a timber 'A' frame but in the event this was demolished due to over-eagerness on the part of the tugs. Fortunately, both the bridge and **Hermes** were undamaged.

(BAE Systems Submarine Solutions)

HMS Hermes makes a fine sight as she steams away from Barrow for the last time on the 17th November 1959 following her trials. ***Hermes*** was laid down in June 1944 but construction was suspended in 1945 when WWII came to an end and she remained on the stocks for seven years taking up valuable berth space awaiting a decision on her future. Once the revised Staff Requirements were made known to the shipyard in 1952, work resumed on her build and she was launched in February 1953. Many advances had been made in aircraft carrier developments during those intervening seven years and in 1954 an extensive modernisation programme was drawn up to accommodate these, the implementation of which took a further four years. Following sea trials she finally left Barrow in November 1959. The all-welded liner ***Orsova*** was constructed alongside ***Hermes*** on the slip. Ironically it was the former, which reputedly brought about an end to the employment of riveters at Barrow, that was scrapped in the early 1970s whereas the riveted ***Hermes*** survives to this day (2008) in the Indian Navy as ***INS Viraat***.

(*The Dock Museum Cat. No. Pr39*)

An analysis of the short service careers of the two Explorer Class experimental submarines is revealing. In the case of **HMS Excalibur**, she spent just under three quarters of the time she was in commission in a state of inactivity. Despite this, she was generally the more reliable of the two boats; her acceptance trials, undertaken between September 1957 to March 1958, were not subject to the same number of breakdowns and interruptions as those of **Explorer**. In fact **Excalibur** was used to complete the first of class deep diving and underwater speed trials which should have been undertaken by her sister. She is shown here berthed in a remote corner of Ramsden Dock, deliberately being kept away from public gaze. She arrived at Barrow in January 1960 to refit. Two months after this photograph was taken work was suspended. It was not completed until May 1962 and just over two years later she paid off for the last time. The boat was returned to Barrow in February 1970 having been sold for scrap to T.W. Ward.

(Ken Royall)

This close-up of the Chilean *Almirante Riveros* provides a good view of her main armament which was unique to these destroyers, having been designed by Vickers at Elswick as a private venture aimed at the foreign market. The four 4-inch 45 calibre Mk.N (R) guns were fitted in single mounts, two superimposed forward and two aft. Entirely automatic, they had a range of 12,500 yards and a maximum elevation of 75 degrees. It was claimed they could achieve a rate of fire of 50rpm although the Admiralty doubted this owing to the lack of a water cooling system. Initially, *Almirante Riveros* and *Almirante Williams* were equipped with the Plessey AWS-1 set but their electronic fit was progressively improved and increased during their long careers which spanned four decades.

(Ken Royall)

HMS Olympus (Yard No. 1060) going down the ways in June 1960, the second of three Oberon Class submarines built at Barrow for the Royal Navy. At the time these submarines were thought to be the finest of their type in the world, being very quiet and thus well-suited to the covert undersea 'battles' of the Cold War. ***Dreadnought*** was launched four months after *Olympus*, heralding a decade when Barrow became increasingly involved with the first generation of nuclear-powered submarines: the Valiant, Resolution and Improved Valiant Classes. The Vickers workforce adapted readily to the monumental technical demands of this task, thus maintaining the company's position as the UK's premier submarine building yard.

(BAE Systems Submarine Solutions)

An historic moment on Trafalgar Day 1960 as H.M. The Queen launches ***HMS Dreadnought***. This fitting name was chosen ahead of ***Vulcan*** and ***Thunder*** to mark a significant milestone in Royal Navy history. The covered building sheds in the background, which had been used during the construction of many wartime boats including ***HMS Upholder***, provide an interesting link with the past. The photograph shows the distinctive shape of the high-performance hull of the submarine with its low length/beam ratio. Despite being the country's leading submarine building and engineering company, constructing ***Dreadnought*** was a considerable achievement for Vickers, the standard of welding alone demanded very high levels of accuracy in order that the boat could meet her specifications including the required diving depth. The apparently relaxed attitude to security surrounding this important event is illustrated by the presence of several private spectator boats in the foreground. *(Ken Royall)*

HMS Dreadnought being towed from the Walney Channel to Devonshire Dock where fitting-out and trials would continue for a further two and a half years. ***Admiralty Floating Dock (AFD) 59*** had been built in fifteen months at Portsmouth Dockyard in preparation for receiving ***Dreadnought***. Large covers would be used in the dock to shroud her from the vagaries of the weather and to allow more sensitive work on the submarine to be carried out away from the public gaze. The bow, prominent in this photograph, was configured to accommodate the large Type 2001 sonar array which was positioned above her six torpedo tubes. The smoothest achievable shape into which the sonar would be fitted was deemed necessary in order to provide laminar flow of water over the sensitive transducers.

(Ken Royall)

The Type 81 frigate **HMS Mohawk** moments after entering Walney Channel on the 5th April 1962, the last of the Tribal Class to be laid down but not the last to complete. She was the only ship of her class to be built at Barrow. The photograph shows her with superstructure blocks and lattice mast in place but she is lacking her funnels, armament and sensors. The Type 81 saw a return to a 'General Purpose' design of frigate, the ships being given 'second-rate' ASW, AA and AD capabilities. The flush deck, with prominent sheer and superstructure extending the full width of the ship, were very much contemporary design features.

(BAE Systems Submarine Solutions)

A fine view of **HMS Dreadnought** on the surface at speed after she had been handed over to the Royal Navy in April 1963. Her Preliminary Sea Trials had commenced in December 1962. Because the build had been subject to delays, the pledge of the then Secretary of State for Defence that **Dreadnought** would go to sea in 1962 had looked increasingly unachievable. However, in the end there was enough water in the Walney Channel to enable the submarine to get out and back during one two-day tidal window. Trials continued post-commissioning and a number of VIPs enjoyed the fact that, at the time, there were no restrictions on the use of full power.

(BAE Systems Submarine Solutions)

The Tribal Class frigate **HMS Mohawk** is apparently externally complete in this photograph despite the fact that she is still in builder's hands. Although she is under her own power, she is being assisted by tugs and is being watched by a number of onlookers on her upper deck. The all-welded, aluminium main mast, although sturdy in appearance, in fact weighed less than the Type 965 long-range surveillance radar aerial it supported. The lattice structure enabled the Type 293Q, sited forward on its own small foremast, to 'see' through the main mast. The Tribals' general purpose capabilities made them useful for peacetime independent patrols and showing the flag duties. *Mohawk*'s 20 year service in the RN ended in 1983. She was the only frigate to be built at Barrow.   *(BAE Systems Submarine Solutions)*

Either **HMS Valiant** or **Warspite** safely afloat with some of the men who helped build her watching proceedings from the slipway. A work-boat is in the process of collecting the large amounts of timber which have been dragged into the water during the launch. These were not only valuable, reusable assets but also hazards to water traffic if not removed. For a while in the mid-1960s it looked as if the tight time-scale for the Polaris submarine programme, for which Barrow was responsible for half, would adversely affect the building of these two submarines. However, as **Valiant** was being used as the prototype for the all-British nuclear propulsion plant, her completion to time became imperative. The case for postponing **Warspite** seemed even stronger but in the event her build was allowed to continue on the grounds that Vickers would need to consolidate its expertise in advance of the full SSBN workload. *(BAE Systems Submarine Solutions)*

The stern of **HMS Valiant** briefly disappears from view while the angle of the cables astern of the fin indicate that the attached drag chains beneath the water are helping to slow the submarine's progress. In the mean time the large launch crew crowd together on the forward casing, most having taken a firm grip on the guard-rails in order to retain their balance. Note the life-belts positioned at intervals in case of an emergency. To outward appearances, **Valiant** was very similar to **Dreadnought**. However, her fore planes were sited further aft to reduce turbulence around the bow sonar while the re-siting of some tanks, in order to obtain a better longitudinal balance, result-ed in a slightly longer and larger submarine.

(Ken Royall)

Valiant was the first all-British nuclear submarine although use was made of American technology learned through the incorporation of the S5W propulsion plant in ***Dreadnought***. However, the Navy wanted the Valiant Class to be considerably quieter than ***Dreadnought***. Therefore, the mounting of the turbines and gearing on 'rafts' in order to reduce the detectable acoustic signal emitted by the vessel caused by the transmission of noise from the machinery to the hull, constituted a significant innovation in the design of these boats. Here ***Valiant***, with three tugs in attendance, is being towed from the slipways towards the Barrow dock system. The boat was four months short of completion when a workman opened a valve allowing 20 tons of water to enter. He claimed to have been given a valve number for ***Warspite***, in an adjacent dry dock, instead of ***Valiant***, the boat he had been working on. A potentially calamitous situation was averted just in time as the submarine listed heavily astern and the level of the dock water came ever closer to the open hatch-way leading to the escape tower.

(Ken Royall)

A fine view of **HMS Osiris** at speed on the surface during her sea trials in early 1964. Despite the fact that Vickers was heavily involved in nuclear submarine building at this time in the 1960s, **Dreadnought** was completing and work on a new class of nuclear boat in the shape of **Valiant** and **Warspite** was underway, this submarine took only 24 months from laying down to completion. It is a testament to the capacity and efficiency of the shipbuilder that the three Barrow Oberons took on average just under two years each to construct compared with nearly three years for the other yards involved in this programme. It also has to be borne in mind that merchant vessels totalling some 170,000 tons were at various stages of completion during the same period. *(BAE Systems Submarine Solutions)*

The absence of workers in this part of the New Assembly Shop would suggest that the photograph was taken probably between the end of the day shift and beginning of the night shift, some time in the mid-1960s. Large numbers of hull sections belonging to the two Resolution Class submarines can be seen at various stages of completion. In the foreground are the formers and cross-bracing jigs used to ensure the circularity of the hull. The vast majority of the pre-fabrication work in view will comprise central units for the boats. However, a fore or aft-end section, with its pronounced taper, can be seen on the right. A mandrel, upon which a hull section could be rotated, is visible in the background.

(BAE Systems Submarine Solutions)

Despite the maze of scaffolding, work on this SSBN, either **Resolution** or **Repulse**, was quite advanced when this photograph was taken. Most of the hull is complete and the fin is in place. The large empty space in the bow is for the sonar transducer which has yet to be fitted. Large sections of temporary roofing, aft of the fin, are at present protecting the reactor compartment from the elements. To the right, early work on another submarine, probably an Improved Valiant or C Class, has commenced. The bright spots inside the hull section are temporary lighting system bulbs.

(BAE Systems Submarine Solutions)

The fact that **HMS Resolution** appears to be lying particularly high in the water in Walney Channel following her launch is probably due to the fact that some of her pre-launch fitting out was behind schedule and she launched lighter in displacement than originally intended. At the time, the SSBN had the distinction of being the largest submarine in the western world. Negotiating the 7,600 tons submarine through the locks at the dock entrance proved hair-raising when she returned from her sea trials. The Commanding Officer (Port), Cdr. Michael Henry, in his capacity as "temporary merchant ship master" while the boat flew the Red Ensign prior to her commissioning, was forced to relieve the local pilot of the conn in order to avoid Resolution's bows being 'landed' on the wooden piles at the lock entrance to the dock system, apparently a practice normally carried out with merchant ships at Barrow in order to swing them into position. The boat was successfully brought into the lock on this occasion, without the aid of tugs, on the very last hour of the flood tide.

(Ken Royall)

HMS Resolution departing Barrow. Her sea trials in 1967 had to conducted within a strict eight week period because the tides would only allow the boat to pass through the lock and into the Walney Channel on a couple of days in June and back again in August. In case bad weather disrupted the programme, it was planned to transport her clear of Barrow on a floating dock and then float her out at sea. In the outcome this was not necessary but ***Resolution*** grounded temporarily in the lock system before the tide rose just sufficiently for her to be moved. It has to be remembered that those responsible were handling the UK's first deterrent submarine, with all its attendant political overtones and with a nuclear reactor which was 'critical' by this stage. The core had been loaded in January 1967 and 'power range test-ed' in nearby Ramsden Dock when the reactor was brought up to a proportion of its full capability.   *(BAE Systems Submarine Solutions)*

The large, temporary cover encircling this nuclear submarine was necessary not only to protect the workers from the elements but also to maintain the constant temperatures required for the specialist welding to be undertaken. However, before units or heavy castings could be welded, a process known as arc-air gouging took place whereby a copper-coated iron rod was used to melt the steel so that it could be cut or shaped to size. The gouged area was then cleaned and buffed with a high-cycle grinder. Prior to the gouging work starting, the surrounding steel had to be preheated to a temperature of 121°C or more. This, with the attendant noise and fumes, and all within the confined space of the boat's hull, made these jobs some of the most unpleasant in the industry at the time. *(BAE Systems Submarine Solutions)*

This stern section of the pressure hull of either **Courageous** or **Churchill** is seen partly inside the New Assembly Shop. It is still supported on wooden timbers on either side and the shipwrights are ensuring that the load is properly distributed before the transporter can take the weight and begin its journey to the slipway and the area known locally as the 'top yard'. The size of these prefabricated sections had steadily increased over the years and, by the time the nuclear programme was underway in the 1960s, the management was concerned to protect some of the underground power systems in the vicinity of the New Assembly Shop. Consequently, steel plates were laid to absorb the movement of the sizes of load that had certainly not been envisaged when the buildings were constructed.

(BAE Systems Submarine Solutions)

The grim faces on the crew members of the tug **Rampside** say it all as she draws away from **HMS Repulse**, firmly stuck on a sandbank in the middle of Walney Channel on her launch day, 4th November 1967. Earlier, the three attendant tugs had failed to secure her in time and **Repulse** had grounded on a falling tide. An eyewitness recalls sheltering behind a funnel on one of the tugs as severed hawsers flew in all directions during the struggle to free the submarine. Aside from the embarrassment of this very public spectacle, it was realised that, if the boat was not refloated within thirty-six hours, the next suitable high tides would be a month later. *(Ken Royall)*

One might assume, at first glance, that this submarine had been beached deliberately and was awaiting the breaker's torch. However, this was the newly-launched **HMS Repulse**, now high and dry in Walney Channel. At least the Head of the SSBN Design Team felt vindicated because his prior calculations had shown that the submarine would remain safely upright in the event of a grounding. Shortly after midnight on the next tide, some thirteen hours after she had drifted onto the sandbank, seven tugs with a combined 10,000bhp managed to free **Repulse** with the cheers of 1,500 spectators ringing in the background. The drama was not quite over as the boat then collided with a dock gate as she was brought round to her fitting-out berth. *(Fred Strike)*

The large crowd of dockyard workers are closely observing the eventful aftermath of the launch of **HMS Repulse** on the 4th November 1967. In the background is the aft section of the hull of **HMS Churchill**, one of three Improved Valiant Class SSNs, two of which were built at Barrow. The photograph affords a good indication of the sheer size of these 3,500 tons submarines when out of the water. It would be another thirteen months before this boat was launched on 20th December 1968. Although the dimensions and hull form of this trio were identical to the earlier Valiants, internally there were upgrades to machinery layout and equipment. *(Ken Royall)*

A prefabricated segment of pressure hull, almost certainly a part of the Improved Valiant Class submarine **HMS Courageous**, leaving the New Assembly Shop on its way to the slipways. The brick building on the left is the old Time Office. The New Assembly Shop at the top yard had been extensively refurbished in the 1950s. New cranes had been installed in order to manoeuvre the increasingly large sections and extensions had been added to the existing building, which was also called the Assembly Shop. However, the issue of ventilation was not addressed at the time. Consequently, all the smoke and noxious fumes produced by the welding, gouging and grinding work tended to become trapped beneath the roof of the shop.

(BAE Systems Submarine Solutions)

The profile of **HMS Churchill** is discernible beneath the scaffolding, staging and covers encircling her hull. This photograph of her on Four Berth, probably taken in 1968, amply illustrates the contrasts in shipbuilding practices at Barrow at the time. Extremely high standards and skills were demanded in order to build a modern, nuclear-powered submarine with a hull strength capable of withstanding high speeds, quite violent manoeuvring and frequent dives to maximum depth. However, a good deal of the work was being still being undertaken in the traditional surroundings of the open slip. The rough and ready condition of the area surrounding *Churchill* and the rust-streaked appearance of parts of her hull seem reminiscent of a previous era.

(BAE Systems Submarine Solutions)

The Valiant Class nuclear-powered submarine **HMS Warspite** leaving Barrow on the 20th November 1968, just short of a month after she had arrived at the yard with a large black tarpaulin covering the fore part of her conning tower. Officially, the explanation was that the boat, while manoeuvring vigorously, had collided with an iceberg and had subsequently rolled twice to excessive angles. However, a collision with a Soviet submarine, or more likely a surface warship, after a lengthy shadowing operation have also been suggested as possible explanations for the damage caused. The fact that **Warspite** was returned to service so quickly is a testament to the efficiency of the Barrow yard and a reflection of the fact that Britain needed this scarce and valuable resource back in action as soon as possible at the height of the Cold War.

(Ken Royall)

A squad of launchway shipwrights are in the process of 'pegging out' a stern section of the Improved Valiant Class submarine **HMS Courageous** on the building berth. The photograph affords a good view of the intricate composition of the keel blocks and packing being built up beneath the boat to hold the hull at exactly the right angle to ensure a smooth launch at a future date. The temporary struts inside the hull are used to maintain its circularity prior to the installation of decks, tanks and other equipment. The empty circle at the centre allowed the entire section to be fitted onto a mandrel, a rotating 'arm' which enabled the superstructure to be revolved in the assembly shop in order to ease the construction process.

(BAE Systems Submarine Solutions)

By all accounts, the distinctive white markings applied to the hull of **HMS Churchill** were only used for this launch and were not matched on her port side. Appropriately, the submarine was named and sent down the ways on the 20th December 1968 by Mrs Mary Soames, the youngest daughter of Sir Winston Churchill. **Churchill** started Contractor's Sea Trials in March 1970 and commissioned the following July. Somewhat unusually, she also underwent a routine docking and maintenance at Barrow the following year. Later the same decade, the boat conducted trials with a prototype pump-jet propulsor in lieu of a propeller, that later became the standard fit on these boats. **Churchill**'s sister, **HMS Courageous**, is to be seen under construction on the right of the photograph.

(Ken Royall)

The Iranian frigates **Rostam** and **Zaal** at their fitting-out berth in late March 1969. **Rostam** had been launched at the Vickers yard in Newcastle and then towed to Barrow for completion. **Zaal** had her superstructure in place when launched about three weeks earlier, including her funnel casing which can now be seen standing on the adjacent quayside. **Rostam**, on the other hand, despite being laid down four months earlier than her sister, is well behind in terms of construction. The four Saam Class frigates, designed as a private venture by Vosper Thornycroft, represented the latest in contemporary western warship design with modern light-weight weaponry, man-power efficient machinery and ongoing maintenance savings made possible through unit replacement methods. **Rostam**, re-named **Sabalan** following the revolution in Iran, was severely damaged by a USN laser-guided bomb in 1988 but was reported back in service three years later. It is unclear whether or not the ship is still in service (2007).

(Ken Royall)

HMS Courageous going down the ways on the 7th March 1970, the second of a pair of Improved Valiant Class boats to be built at Barrow, the third, **HMS Conqueror**, having been constructed at Cammell Laird, Birkenhead. This close up gives a good indication of the very high standards of welding which produced the quality finish on her cylindrical hull. **Courageous** was the first SSN to be refitted with the Type 2020 bow-mounted long-range active/passive sonar and also received the American built long-range anti-ship weapon, Sub-Harpoon, in Autumn 1981. Although she arrived off the Falklands in late May 1982, a lack of suitable targets denied her the opportunity to fire this formidable sea-skimming weapon. *(MoD/Crown Copyright*

There is a discernibly relaxed atmosphere on the quarterdeck of the Iranian frigate **Zaal** with several personnel taking advantage of the sunny weather during her contractor's sea trials, probably in early 1971. This photograph affords a good view of the ship's armament: the Mk.5 DP 4.5in gun forward of the bridge, the Limbo Mk10 ASW mortar in its well aft, the Sea Cat SAM launcher on the small platform just forward of it and, finally, the twin 35mm Oerlikon Bührle mounting on the port quarter. The development of the Olympus marine gas turbine, with a rating in excess of 22,500hp, had enabled the designers to use this as the main source of power instead of as a boost system used in conjunction with conventional steam turbines. A CODOG (combined diesel or gas) arrangement was provided with two Paxman Ventura diesels fitted for cruising at 17.5 knots.

(BAE Systems Submarine Solutions)

Final preparations are underway here for the launch of the Type 42 destroyer **HMS Sheffield** by H.M. The Queen. Two months earlier, an explosion had occurred between bulkheads 43 and 53 in the double bottom due to a welding accident. The hull was also being zinc-sprayed at the time as anti-corrosion protection for fresh water storage. Two men had been killed and a third injured and it resulted in considerable damage to the engine room of the ship in addition to a 25-foot split in the hull. This incident threatened to delay not only the launch but also the rest of the Type 42 construction programme at Barrow; **ARA Hercules** was due to be laid down on the same slipway immediately after **Sheffield** had vacated it. In the event, the Argentine Navy agreed to allow the prefabricated stern section of their destroyer to be used as a replacement for part of **Sheffield's** damaged hull, in order not to disrupt the schedule.

(Ken Royall)

HMS Sheffield shortly after arrival at the fitting-out berth on 10th June 1971, the day of her launch. Externally, apart from the funnel and two masts, little else has been added to the basic superstructure. Note that she lacks her distinctive funnel exhaust ducts at this stage, a feature that made **Sheffield** unique among the RN Type 42s. This period of her construction was greatly assisted by the modular nature of much of the equipment involved, including the main machinery, armament and radars. Nevertheless, as first of class, the destroyer's fitting-out was a protracted affair, taking over three years to complete.

(Ken Royall)

This photograph was taken just after **HMS Swiftsure** had been secured to her attendant tugs in Walney Channel on her launch day, 7th May 1971. It is a reflection of the times that the vast majority of the launch crew seen in this photograph have donned life-jackets. Company workboats will soon begin the task of clearing the assorted wooden packing which the submarine dragged into water in the process of being launched. Nameship of her class, *Swiftsure* was the first of a second generation of British nuclear submarines whose design was the result of a careful evaluation of past experience gained when building and operating the two Valiant Classes. For instance, the hull was made very nearly cylindrical throughout its length in order to eliminate contractions that had reduced 'fatigue life' in the earlier boats. *Swiftsure* undertook sea trials in the Autumn of 1972 and finally sailed from Barrow on 2nd May 1973 to enter operational service.

(Ken Royall)

The initial order for two Oberon Class submarines for the Brazilian Navy was announced in August 1969, a third was to follow three years later. This is the first of the trio, *Humaita*, in Buccleuch Dock in June 1972. The Type 42 destroyer *HMS Sheffield* is berthed astern. The boat is roughly half way through her fitting out programme; it was to be another eight months before she commenced contractor's sea trials. Superficially, *Humaita* appears to be in a fairly advanced stage of construction but it is clear from the amount of cabling being run from ashore into her engine compartments that there is a good deal of internal work being carried out. The submarine's Admiralty Standard Range diesel engines were manufactured by Vickers while the glass fibre laminate fin and casing were produced by a subsidiary, Slingsby Sailplanes Ltd. of Kirkbymoorside.

(Ken Royall)

The Brazilian submarine *Tonelero* ready to be launched on November 22nd 1972. Near disaster was to strike the following October when, within weeks of completion, a serious fire destroyed the Control Room centre section of the boat. The subsequent enquiry ruled that set procedures had not been followed and the fire was started when an atomised spray of hydraulic oil was ignited by a welder's arc. The night shift was swiftly evacuated but the resulting inferno quickly consumed local reserves of CO_2 and extra supplies had to be brought from distant Carlisle before the blaze could be brought under control. *Tonelero* had to be fitted with a replacement section and new equipment at Chatham Dockyard owing to pressure on the existing workload at Barrow. Consequently, she did not complete until September 1978.

(Ken Royall)

It is 22nd February 1974 and **HMS Cardiff** has just been launched from the berth immediately adjacent to **HMS Invincible**, pictured above. Unsurprisingly, work has been temporarily suspended on the carrier and the workforce have taken advantage of available deck space on three levels in order to watch the Type 42 destroyer take to the water. It appears that, at this stage, roughly seven months into build, quite a lot of progress has been made on the hull of the ship. The design policy emphasised large internal volume, thereby allowing all equipment to be easily removed. This proved invaluable in the case of **Invincible's** heavy gearboxes which were fitted before the ship was launched. These items proved defective on more than one occasion during the build but were skilfully removed each time, leaving a gaping hole in the ship's side for months on end.

(Ken Royall)

Riachuelo, the last of the trio to be built for Brazil, lifted in *AFD 19* in Devonshire Dock on 7th September 1975, presumably to enable her lower hull to be examined following her launch the previous day. The fin of a nuclear submarine, probably *HMS Superb*, can be just be made out in the larger floating dock, *AFD 59*, visible in the background. Within ten years, this end of Devonshire Dock would be unrecognisable following the construction of the gigantic Devonshire Dock Hall and attendant synchronized shiplift. *Riachuelo* duly commissioned at Barrow in March 1977 before departing for South America the following July. *(Ken Royall)*

The launch crew on the Israeli submarine ***INS Gal*** perch rather precariously on the boat's casing as she lists heavily to starboard following her launch in December 1975. At the time, some onlookers claimed that the retaining studs on the bow cradle had sheared during her launch, causing excessive movement. The official explanation, however, pointed to incorrect ballasting. The three Type 540 submarines were built as the result of a joint, private venture between Vickers and a German naval architect from IKL Lübeck and were based on the successful Type 206 then in service with the Bundesmarine. The contract for the construction of the boats was highly controversial and diplomatically sensitive. WEU treaty limits prevented Germany from exporting submarines over 350 tons to non-NATO members while the Germans themselves had a strict policy on the non-supply of arms to an area of tension (particularly the Middle East). However, the fact that the submarines would be built in the UK and only the propulsion units would be German, allowed the project to go ahead because, it was argued, the Germans were supplying 'submarine parts' only. Much of the other equipment, including the weapons systems, was British made and the sonar was supplied by the Netherlands.

(Ken Royall)

An incomplete **HMS Cardiff** leaving Barrow under tow on the 2nd February 1976 bound for Swan Hunter. The latter yard had agreed to a sub-contract by Vickers to complete the ship on the Tyne. *Cardiff* was one of five Batch I Type 42s ordered in 1971. She was laid down in June of that year and launched in November 1972. However, the yard at the time was heavily committed to the Swiftsure Class SSN programme, the building of the carrier *Invincible* and other construction work for foreign navies. As a result, there was a shortage of skilled labour in certain critical trades. It is clear from her external appearance that little work had been carried out on *Cardiff* in nearly four years and it is unsurprising that she was destined to endure the longest construction time of any ship of her class. However, it was reckoned that the delay would have been greater had *Cardiff* remained at Barrow.

(Ken Royall)

A very smart looking ***ARA Hercules*** returning to Barrow from sea trials on the 9th May 1976 the day before her official completion. Although she commissioned in July of that year, further operational sea training in the UK meant that she didn't arrive in Argentina until August 1977. She had been laid down in June 1971 shortly after the same slipway had been vacated by ***HMS Sheffield***. Vickers had offered three designs and part of the resulting contract agreement for the Type 42 enabled the Argentinians to familiarise themselves enough with the latest construction techniques for ***Hercules*** sistership, ***Santisima Trinidad***, to be built in Argentina. *(Ken Royall)*

The 4,400 tons **HMS Superb** in June 1976, some nineteen months after her launch. She is under tow and has just passed through the narrow entrance between Devonshire Dock and Buccleuch Dock beneath the raised section of the High Level Bridge. The distinctive 250-tons capacity crane on the right (since demolished) dominated the Barrow skyline for most of the 20th Century. It was originally constructed to lift large guns and mountings aboard battleships alongside the fitting-out berth beneath. Prefabricated hull sections, probably from one of the follow-on 'S' Class boats, can just be seen on the quayside between the crane and the bridge.

(MoD/Crown Copyright)

This semi-deserted scene is in striking contrast to the usual crowded slipway prior to a launching. The 540 Class *Tanin* (Crocodile) is about to be sent down the slipway on October 25th 1976 by the wife of the Israeli Ambassador. Such was the fear of an Arab boycott that it was only some time after construction had started on the three submarines that Vickers publicly admitted that they were being built for Israel. Unlike other vessels, details about their movements and trials were not published in the local papers and it is clear that the ceremony about to begin is for a selected audience only. Later, a road accident, which resulted in the deaths of three crew members, returning to Barrow by minibus, drew unwanted publicity and served to aggravate an already delicate international situation. This led to the third boat, Rahav, being constructed on a pontoon in Buccleuch Dock in order to avoid further attention. Five years earlier, there had been ambitious plans by Vickers and the German firm Howaldtswerke for a 'long term programme' and the 'possible division of the world into two zones for manufacturing and marketing' small submarines.   *(Ken Royall)*

First of class **HMS Invincible** sliding into the water on a very wet 3rd May 1977, the only one of the three aircraft carriers of her class to be built at Barrow. Note the small group on the bridge roof who have taken up a unique vantage point from which to experience the launch. Vickers was awarded the contract by virtue of the fact that they were the only UK company at the time with the resources to develop the Ship Department's design, principally because of their large white-collar, technical work force which had been built up for the nuclear submarine programmes the previous decade. *Invincible* completed in July 1980 almost exactly seven years after she had been laid down.

(Ken Royall)

The penultimate Swiftsure Class submarine *HMS Spartan* ploughing sternwards into Walney Channel on the 7th April 1978, just under two years after she had been laid down. Her sister *HMS Splendid* is occupying the adjacent berth with her midships and stern sections already in position. The smart, modern building to the left with the tall chimney is SMITE (Submarine Machinery Installation and Testing Establishment). The Admiralty Development Establishment (ADEB) at Barrow, whose origins dated from the HTP era of the 1950s, was used at the time to assemble and test the Swiftsure Class non-nuclear machinery. The problem was that ADEB was housed a considerable distance from the building slips. The SMITE building was the replacement and it was finished in time to test the machinery of the last Swiftsure Class boat, *HMS Splendid*, and the follow-on Trafalgar Class.

(Ken Royall)

This photograph of the carrier **HMS Invincible** was taken in July 1978, fourteen months after her launch. Her 'ski jump' is at an early stage of construction and while her Sea Dart launcher has been fitted just forward of the flight deck, it is covered with a tarpaulin. The prominent blast deflector for the missile has not been shipped yet. One of her Type 910 Sea Dart tracker radar is also in place just forward of the bridge, again shrouded from view. In common with other vessels at this stage of completion, *Invincible*'s appearance has deteriorated somewhat since her launch when she would have been given a fresh coat of paint. The patches of darker paint on her hull forward of the superstructure are where some, but not all, of the temporary drag plates used at her launch have been removed.

(Ken Royall)

HMS Invincible undergoing inclination tests in Buccleuch Dock on the 3rd March 1979. Perhaps surprisingly, given her appearance, the ship is still fifteen months away from commissioning. However, closer inspection reveals that her ski-jump ramp, for example, is under construction. This took the form of a 47-ton light steel structure which was welded to the flight deck. The requirement to limit the cost and displacement of this class but at the same time to ensure that the flight deck was long enough to operate Sea Harriers, was a concern and resulted in an innovative design using a much lighter alloy and no armour. Construction was not straightforward either and some horizontal stiffeners had to be added during the build to counter buckling problems. The result was a ship with high volume for its tonnage and a high beam-to-draft ratio in order to achieve stability.

(Ken Royall)

HMS Splendid, the sixth and last Swiftsure Class boat to be built at Barrow, enters the water for the first time on 5th October 1979. She was launched into Walney Channel by the wife of C-in-C Fleet, Admiral Sir James Eberle. Note the temporary platform above the boat's casing and the heavy shackles and cables used to attach ***Splendid*** to the drag chains on either side. The launch crew can also been seen crowded together forward of the fin; the rudimentary barriers and the absence of hard hats are symptomatic of a relaxed attitude towards Health and Safety even five years after the 1974 Act. The building berth to the right is already occupied by Yard No. 1100, later to become ***HMS Trafalgar***.

(MoD/Crown Copyright)

This photograph affords a close view of the standing ways down which **HMS Trafalgar** travelled during her launch a short while earlier. Piles of the drag chains which helped slow the submarine's progress as she entered the water are nearby, ready to be collected. In the background the boat lies afloat in the Walney Channel for the first time and her launch crew are hard at work securing her fore and aft to attendant tugs. A serious accident had been avoided earlier when one of the tug skippers noticed that the pilot had omitted to give the order to release the last cable. The task of releasing the heavy steel slip proved to be a difficult and potentially dangerous operation as all the strain was on the side of the drag plate.

(MoD/Crown Copyright)

The destroyer **HMS Manchester** leaving Barrow for the last time. The three Batch 3 Type 42s, featuring stretched bows and increased beam, were ordered during 1978/9 and **Manchester** herself was laid down in November 1978, Vickers having been chosen as the lead yard. Owing to their long experience and expertise, they managed to complete the destroyer to this new design in four and a half years. However, while other British warship building firms working at the time on the Batch 3 ships had invested money in large, covered construction berths which enabled work to proceed independently of the weather, **HMS Manchester** was built on a conventional, open slipway. Note that she is still sporting a pre-Falklands paint scheme in this photograph taken on 15th November 1982. *(Ken Royall)*

HMS Turbulent secured to tugs following her launch on a chilly December day in Walney Channel. Some members of the launch crew gathered on the temporary sponson on the forward casing appear ready to disembark. ***Turbulent***, Yard No. 1101, was the second of the seven Trafalgar Class submarines, all of which were built by Vickers at Barrow. The necessity to make these boats as quiet as possible resulted in extensive tests and research by the MoD, Vickers and the many equipment suppliers. It was claimed that tests on the noise ranges suggested that this class were quieter than the Oberon Class SSKs, which constituted an important breakthrough in nuclear submarine technology.

(MoD/Crown Copyright)

HMS Trafalgar on a misty day in the Clyde in February 1984 while on her sea trials. Although it had been less than a quarter of a century since the launch of ***Dreadnought***, the RN was about to receive into service its fourth new class of SSN. Each class had demonstrated an incremental improvement in design: perhaps the most obvious visual difference between this boat and the earlier Valiant Class is the apparent absence of foreplanes. These had been re-sited below the waterline and were only spread when dived and at slow speed. On the surface and at speed she presented a highly hydrodynamic shape. ***HMS Trafalgar*** was the first submarine whose machinery had not been tested with a full scale wooden mock-up. A one-fifth scale model was used instead which was scanned by telescope, the results being passed to a computer.

(MoD/Crown Copyright)

HMS Upholder on the synchro-lift outside Devonshire Dock Hall in December 1986, commencing the long process of being lowered into the water. The boat has been manoeuvred from the transfer position just inside the entrance to the Hall by the remotely operated transfer cars or bogies. These have now been detached, leaving **Upholder** supported on its cradles. The 162 metre shiplift is worked by 108 electric winches, each with a lifting capacity of 224 tons. The hydrodynamic shape with its characteristic tear-drop hull made these submarines closely resemble contemporary SSNs. Like the nuclear boats, they were constructed in sections using high-tensile steel, stiffened with HT steel frames. The photograph affords an excellent view of the submarine's Type 2040 bow cylindrical array, masked in the photograph by a steel cover. The three layers of transducers set in 48 staves, provide both intercept and range data.

(BAE Systems Submarine Solutions)

The temporary platform fitted over the bow of *HMS Upholder* allows the launch crew sufficient space to adjust the tension on the hawsers which maintain the boat's position as she is carefully floated off her cradles that now rest on the shiplift at the bottom of the dock. Behind her, the northern flank of Devonshire Dock Hall is still under construction. One of the great advantages of this type of launch has been the avoidance of what is referred to as 'weld duplication'. Weight restrictions mean that no more than 75% of a boat's equipment can be installed when it is 'dynamically' launched, leading to the necessity afterwards to open up completed hull and bulkhead welds, install equipment at the fitting out berth and then re-weld.

(BAE Systems Submarine Solutions)

HMS Triumph leaving her fittingout berth in Devonshire Dock in November 1991, less than a week before commissioning. The last Trafalgar Class submarine to be built, she was also the first to benefit from the less spectacular but (for the vessel) considerably less stressful shiplift launch following her construction inside Devonshire Dock Hall. Despite this technological milestone, there was embarrassment for the yard when it was discovered that one of the hull sections of the submarine had been inserted and welded into position upside down. Fortunately, in terms of time and cost, the framing was of sufficient thickness and no remedial action was necessary.

(Ken Royall)

HMS Talent entering the dock system from Walney Channel on the day of her launch in 1988. She was destined to be the last submarine to be subjected to a dynamic launch. Although it normally lasts less than a minute, a dynamic launch imposes considerable stress on a vessel, particularly at the point when the stern is afloat and the weight is on the bow which is still on the slipway, supported only by the bow cradle. The prominent piece of advertising for VSEL proved unpopular and was not repeated in this form at subsequent events. HRH The Princess Royal launched the boat on a particularly dismal 15th April although the weather seems to have cleared somewhat by the time this photograph was taken.

(Ken Royall)

This photograph captures an important event in history for VSEL, the Royal Navy and the country at large as the 15,900 tons (dived) SSBN *HMS Vanguard* emerges from the cavernous Devonshire Dock Hall on March 4th 1992. Watched by a large crowd of company employees, the boat was rolled out on 88 electrically operated transfer cars at a steady rate of one metre per minute while a band played music from '*2001 – A Space Odyssey*'. This operation took two and a half hours and once on the shiplift the launch itself, or 'dunking', took a further one and a half hours to complete. The execution of this controversial project was described at the time as "the biggest, most complex and expensive in Western Europe". Vickers worked in close cooperation with the American Electric Boat Company and some of the initial design work had commenced as far back as the early 1970s.

(Ken Royall)

The second of the four Vanguard Class boats, **HMS Victorious**, being returned to her berth in Devonshire Dock following a period of sea trials. She is being assisted by Vickers' workboats and there are lines fore and aft to the accompanying tugs. Views of these submarines leaving or returning to Barrow, without their four tugs lashed alongside, are rare. However, the tugs had to detach in order to allow the boats to pass through the narrow entrance to Devonshire Dock beneath Michaelson Road. The revolutionary shape of the hull is evident here while the personnel on the casing and the fin give a good indication of the sheer size of these SSBNs. **HMS Victorious**, which was longer under construction than her three sisters, was five months away from commissioning when this photograph was taken in August 1994.   *(Ken Royall)*

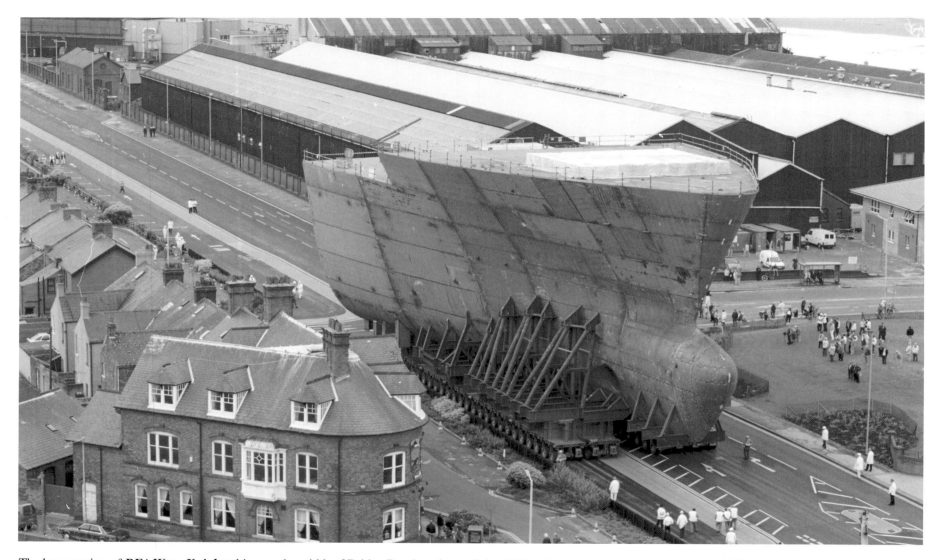

The bow section of **RFA Wave Knight** taking up the width of Bridge Road on the 1st July 1999 on its journey from Devonshire Dock Hall to the new entrance to the slipway. The prominent, dark painted sheds in the background are the old 'Platers' and 'Markers-Off' (or 'Liners-Off') Lofts which have since been demolished while the bow-fronted brick building in the foreground is The Crow's Nest Public House. Contracts to build the two Wave Class fleet tankers were placed with VSEL in March 1997. Construction of her sistership **RFA Wave Ruler** was subsequently switched to Govan, a move which both saved the firm's Glasgow yard from closure and prevented construction delays. A symbolic keel-laying ceremony for **Wave Knight** took place on the 22nd May 1998 in DDH, the same day as the LPD **HMS Albion**. The twelve block modules which made up the Royal Fleet Auxiliary were largely outfitted within the confines of the hall before being transported to the specially created 'superberth'.

(BAE Systems Submarine Solutions)

A spectacular view of **RFA Wave Knight** taking to the water for the first time on the 29th September 2000. Surprisingly perhaps, it had been over 85 years since the last RFA had been launched at the yard. Walney Channel required extensive dredging for the occasion and due care had to be taken with the launch date to avoid disturbing the gulls' breeding season. Although the method of construction and the sympathetic approach to the local ecology would have been unrecognisable when the tanker **Santa Margherita** was launched in May 1915, the two ships share similarities. Both were built to Admiralty/MoD designs and while **Santa Margherita** was equipped with diesel engines and electric auxiliaries, **Wave Knight** has four diesel generators connected to an electric main propulsion motor. *(BAE Systems Submarine Solutions)*

127

The bow unit of **HMS Bulwark** exiting through the western doors of the Devonshire Dock Hall on its way to the building berth. Five of the seven block modules which constituted the LPD's hull were assembled in DDH. Some weighing up to 2,400 tons each, represented the bulkiest loads ever transported on a UK public highway. **Bulwark** is dwarfing a section of the hull of the submarine **HMS Astute**. This photograph was taken in February 2001, shortly after the boat's keel-laying ceremony, hence the Union Flag, company banner and ship's badge. Less than a year after this important landmark, the entire Astute Class programme was in disarray as the company and the MoD finally came to terms with the huge cost and time overruns which had afflicted this project, together with a critical haemorrhaging of specialist skills from the workforce caused by the gap in orders since the completion of the Vanguard Class.

(BAE Systems Submarine Solutions)

A crowded and busy scene inside Devonshire Dock Hall during the building of the two Albion Class amphibious assault ships with several modules at different stages of construction. The facility's two high level cranes are capable of 150 tonne lifts; the large sub-unit suspended here allows a unique sight of some interior compartments before they are hidden from view. A further advantage of the advanced assembly technique used by BAE Systems is that smaller units can be inverted in order to minimize the necessity for awkward overhead welding tasks and to facilitate painting. Unobstructed access to the hull means that some large items of equipment, in this instance the ship's main machinery which can be seen under covers in the left foreground, can be 'fleeted in' and, importantly, pre-tested prior to the hull being closed up.

(BAE Systems Submarine Solutions)

Although discussions about replacements for the Fearless Class LPDs had begun in the mid 1980s, it was July 1996 before a £429 million contract was signed with VSEL for the design and build of **HM ships Albion** and **Bulwark**. Two factors caused the in-service dates for both vessels to slip. Firstly, in the late 1990s, the firm was involved in three MoD orders in addition to the LPD programme: the Astute, the Vanguard and the Auxiliary Oiler projects. Secondly, the new CAD (Computer Assisted Design) package faltered badly when required simultaneously to cope with the LPD and Wave Class workloads with consequent engineering congestion in the shipyard. This is **HMS Albion** launching on an overcast and damp day in early March 2001. The small group of employees on the bridge wing do not appear overly elated by this rare event in contrast to earlier photographs of big ship launches into Walney Channel.

(BAE Systems Submarine Solutions)

Work is underway here on completing the superstructure of **HMS Bulwark**. The seven block modules have been welded together and the entire hull has been painted. A mobile crane is currently in the process of lifting part of the bridge structure into place. Internally, work is continuing on installing equipment, cabling, fixtures and welding or fastening pipe joints. Despite the sophistication of modern construction methods, this ship would still undergo a traditional dynamic launch with all the attendant problems of calculating the forces and stresses on the hull during its brief journey to the water. It is interesting to note that, although the keel is held firmly in position at the bows, the stern of the vessel is supported on less substantial looking concrete pillars, reflecting both the fact that there is comparatively little weight in this part of the ship at this stage in her construction and her contemporary, flat-bottomed design.

(*BAE Systems Submarine Solutions*)

The 19,500 tons full load **HMS Bulwark** dominates the Barrow skyline in this photograph taken from the far side of Walney Channel, probably in Autumn 2001. Final preparations for her launch on the 15th November appear to be underway; note the cables already attached to the drag chains on the port side. The temporary viewing stands for the launch party are to be seen under construction beneath the bows of the vessel. **Bulwark** herself has received a fresh coat of paint in advance of the ceremony and, in time-honoured fashion, so has the white stern launch cradle. In contrast with earlier launches of this kind, the ship's superstructure is largely in place with the notable absence of the electronic equipment on the three masts.

(BAE Systems Submarine Solutions)

This photograph of Buccleuch Dock on a misty day in late 2002 shows a loaded LCU Mk10 entering the flooded stern dock of **HMS Albion**. In this part of the commissioning trials programme, both unladen and laden landing craft were manoeuvred in and out of the dock in order to measure handling arrangements on board the ship. Once inside, the vehicles, including Challenger Tanks, were unloaded and undertook a series of manoeuvring serials before disembarkation. As part of the same programme, the deck davits were used to raise and lower the smaller LCVP Mk5 craft. Although these particular first of class trials were completed satisfactorily, the ship's in-service date at this stage had slipped further behind schedule and **Albion** was not expected to join the frontline fleet before July 2003.

(BAE Systems Submarine Solutions)

The submarine *Ursula*, soon to be renamed *HMCS Corner Brook*, undergoing diving trials in Devonshire Dock prior to her naming and acceptance ceremony which took place in February 2003. In comparison with two of her sisters, this boat's re-activation process was comparatively incident-free. *HMS Ursula* was built by Cammell Laird at Birkenhead and commissioned in June 1992. Less than two years later she was laid up with the rest of the class in Buccleuch Dock on a care and maintenance basis pending sale, following the governments's decision to dispense with the RN's non-nuclear submarine force. In 1998 it was announced that Canada had acquired the four boats and VSEL was awarded a £100 million contract to include the re-activation work together with the provision of spares and training for the crews.

(BAE Systems Submarine Solutions)

The 235-tonne bow section of **HMS Ambush** moving at a steady 2.5 miles per hour the quarter-mile distance along Bridge Road from the New Assembly Shop to Devonshire Dock Hall on a 48-wheeled Scheurle transporter in May 2006. This close-up affords a good view of the latest Q1N quenched and tempered steel selected for the pressure hull. Although high strength steel of this type has been in use on RN submarines for the last fifty years, the first material employed, QT35, was susceptible to lamellar tearing owing to its high sulphur and phosphorus contents. Gas shielded, flux cored arc and submerged arc welding techniques have been used by BAE Systems on this class; a computerized system called the 'Weld Management System' individually records all major structural welds, the data including input on material, thickness, type of weld prep together with NDE (Non-Destructive Examination) requirements. The prominent white-painted markings criss-crossing the hull are applied to protect the NDE.

(BAE Systems Submarine Solutions)

A fine view, looking west, of the interior of Devonshire Dock Hall in May 2006. The clean and organised state of the working environment is in marked contrast to earlier photographs of the outside construction berths. Likewise, uniform hard hats among the staff have replaced the cloth caps of old. *HMS Astute* is on the South build line. Despite being festooned with staging, scaffolding and testing equipment, she has been externally 'physically complete' since December 2005 when the final butt weld brought together sections 7 and 8 of the submarine. On the right is the bow section of the second boat of the Astute Class, *HMS Ambush*. The white canvas screen in the foreground is masking the area where sensitive work on the bow array, which forms part of the Type 2076 integrated sonar suite, is being carried out. The domed shaped module, currently on its transporter in the transfer position, is intended for the third of class, *HMS Artful*.

(BAE Systems Submarine Solutions)

HMS Astute finally emerging from Devonshire Dock Hall on the 8 June 2007 some three years later than planned. A fault with the syncro-lift meant that the slow process of lowering the boat into the water had to be abandoned. Problems with damaged turbo-generators and other quality control issues with supplied components resulted in further programme slippage and, consequently, *Astute* is not scheduled to be handed over to the Royal Navy until 2009. In the mean time, although the order for the fourth boat in the class, *HMS Audacious*, was placed in May 2007, doubts remain about the future of what the 1998 Strategic Defence Review originally intended to be a 10-strong SSN force.

Inevitably, a major factor is the soaring cost of these highly sophisticated and advanced submarines. A House of Commons Defence Committee Report, published in 2008, stated that the four Astute Class boats would cost £3.79bn against an initial budget of £2.58bn, amounting to a 47 per cent increase.

(BAE Systems Submarines)

Index